Dartmoor
Trail and Fell Running

Colin Kirk-Potter

www.pesdapress.com

First published in Great Britain 2023 by Pesda Press
Tan y Coed Canol
Ceunant
Caernarfon
Gwynedd
LL55 4RN

© Copyright 2023 Colin Kirk-Potter

Maps by Bute Cartographics
Contains Ordnance Survey data © Crown copyright and database right 2023

ISBN: 9781906095840

The Author has asserted his rights under the Copyright, Designs
and Patents Act, 1988, to be identified as Author of this Work.
All rights reserved. No part of this publication may be reproduced, stored in a retrieval system, or transmitted, in any form or by any means, electronic, mechanical, photocopying, recording or otherwise, without the prior written permission of the publisher.

Printed and bound in Poland, www.hussarbooks.pl

To my wife Laura, for understanding and supporting my obsession and passion for running.

About the Author

Colin is the director of Run Venture Ltd, a running shop and café on the western fringes of Dartmoor, and regularly uses his skills as a qualified Mountain Leader and coach to guide runners across the national park. He has an in-depth knowledge of Dartmoor as a runner, walker and as a former Royal Marine (the moor being a favourite training ground upon which to train the elite, combat troops).

He has completed many of the top fell races, including: the self-navigating, UK Mountain Trail in the Lake District, two Bob Graham rounds, the 105 mile Ultra Trail du Mont Blanc in Europe, and numerous mountain marathons which involve running and navigating in remote areas over two days.

This is his first book, although he has written for local publications and national running magazines.

Colin at a trail race – events.photo-fit.com

Acknowlegements

Without the Royal Marines I might have never even have set foot on what I believe is the best National Park in the country. The men I served alongside shaped my personality and in a roundabout way influenced the style of my writing. To all, serving, former, and those no longer with us; thank you Royal.

The last word has to be for Laura, aka Mary Poppins. Laura not only understands my obsession and passion, but supports it. When I had the idea for the book, in true Mary Poppins style she told me that with the right amount of imagination, anything is possible. Laura has always provided me with an honest guide to life, with the importance of kindness, responsibility, integrity, and the capacity to enjoy life no matter what.

Photographic Acknowlegements

All photographs by the author except where otherwise acknowledged in the captions by the use of the photographers initials or company name.

AF = Adharanand Finn
MB = Mark Bullock
MBa = Mike Barber
ML = Mark Locket

RR = Rob Richards
SW = Sam Waddy
SQ = Stuart Queen

Contents

Dedication	3
About the Author	4
Photographic Acknowlegements	4
Contents	5
Introduction	6
How to Use this Book	8
Running Safely on Dartmoor	11
The Countryside Code	13
Clothing and Equipment	15

NORTH WEST — 25

1 Meldon Reservoir Loop	27
2 The Roof of Devon	31
3 The Great Links Flyer	37
4 Merrivale – Up Past the 'Giants Tummy	41
5 Peter Tavy High Ground	45
6 Okehampton to the Moor and Back	51
7 Belstone Horseshoe	55

SOUTH WEST — 59

8 The Dewer to Pay	61
9 Ditsworthy Warren House	65
10 Crazy Well Loop	69
11 The Neolithic Route	73
12 Burrator Horseshoe	77
13 Princetown and the Aqueduct	81
14 Princetown to Burrator and Back	85

NORTH EAST — 89

15 Fingle Bridge and Castle Drogo	91
16 A Pilgrimage to Jay's Grave	95
17 Far from the Madding Crowd – Haytor	101
18 Moretonhampstead Loop	105
19 Hameldown Hammer	109
20 The Hobbit Half Marathon	113

SOUTH EAST — 119

21 Antique Commuters Break – Ashburton	121
22 North from Ivybridge	125
23 Dartmoor's Snowdon	129
24 Tour of the Dart	133
25 South Brent Bimble	139

CENTRAL — 145

26 Princetown Dash	147
27 Wistman's 'Spooky' Wood	151
28 Gunpowder, Treason and Plot	155
29 Long Circuit South from Postbridge	161

LONGER EXCURSIONS — 165

30 Dartmoor – Top to Bottom	167
31 The Dartmoor 600s	175

Index	181

Introduction

Dartmoor ... 365 square miles of stunning moorland, largely untouched by the community of local, trail runners, let alone those from further afield! Whereas the city half marathons of Exeter and Plymouth sell out in hours and attract up to two thousand entries each, local Dartmoor trail races average about a tenth of that number. Maybe it is because of its legendary reputation of bottomless, peat bogs and mires. Perhaps it is the remote, rocky outcrops known as 'tors' which can be up to three miles from any civilisation, or a perceived lack of recognisable paths that deter the otherwise avid trail warrior. More simply, it might just be because that despite apps, GPS gadgets and computer software, there has never been a specific, trail running guidebook for Dartmoor.

Trail running is rapidly becoming one of the fastest growing sports in the world; the South West, and indeed the whole of the United Kingdom. There are trail running events in abundance, and their unique selling points are their sense of adventure and the chance to get out of the city and run wild. Dartmoor National Park is such a place, but knowing where to run, which routes take in the best scenery, which parts are not to be missed, is often key to enjoying a run on the trails.

Running on Dartmoor scares some people. That sounds like an exaggeration but, talking to many of the local runners, I find that they are afraid of getting lost, or getting injured – and scared that their tech gadget will show a slower pace than they are used to on their usual road runs!

Running is a broad church and encompasses everything from a 100m sprint to a 100 mile plus ultra, on different surfaces from the rubber crumb of a track to the thin, mountain ridges of the Italian Alps. Jumping out the front door and going for a run around the roads, lanes, city, towns, and villages where

Introduction

Bellever Tor at dawn (Route 29) – SW

most of us live is easy. It is within our comfort zone. We don't have to think, we can just run and tick off the miles. For many, that is their thing, and I am not one to say otherwise. However, going for a run on the paths, 'trods' (faint, thin tracks often made by animals and / or humans, literally trodden into the ground) and trails of a national park such as Dartmoor, is a different experience compared to that of a road run. Yes, it is still classed as running but it is different. The terrain underfoot is different, the ups and downs are different. The experience is different. It is the same with cycling; where there is road cycling, mountain biking, downhill, stunt, BMX, touring, the list goes on. Yes, they are all on a bike, but different.

So what qualifies me to write this book? I have lived, worked, trained, and raced on Dartmoor for over 20 years, the first 17 years as a Royal Marine Commando. The national park provided the perfect, training environment for the elite unit, then for an international trail running competitor, and more recently in my role as a qualified Mountain Leader and running guide, working from my own running shop and hub on the edge of the moor. I can safely say that I am well acquainted with the Dartmoor trail and fell running scene. Having ran trails on three continents, Dartmoor is still, in my mind, running's best kept secret!

This book, *Dartmoor Trail and Fell Running*, outlines some of the best trail running routes the national park has to offer. Whether it be climbing over the rugged, northern 600m tors, or tearing along an 18th century leat from a Napoleonic prison, this off-road running guide has options to suit all tastes and abilities.

Its aim is to highlight the best of what Dartmoor has to offer for the runner. Whether you are an experienced weather-beaten trail warrior looking to explore a different set of trails, or a lean, mean road running machine keen to mix it up and add a bit of trail work to your training.

The routes included in this guide are not by any means the limit. Indeed, there is an abundance of other routes available, but understanding where to run is often a barrier. This book is just your starting point.

How to Use this Book

This book is only a guide, and although the routes contain a detailed description and a map to accompany them, they are no substitute for a map and compass, and the ability to use both.

I would not expect for one moment that you would take this book in one hand while running full pelt over the tussocks of Dartmoor in the depths of winter, hoping to read the finer details of route choice. Ideally, I would select a route from the book prior to the run, annotate a map and take that. I have known some folk print off the directions I have sent them and carry them in a waterproof map case along with their map or, photograph it on to their smart phones.

The first time you run an unfamiliar route, do not expect fast times compared to those of your usual runs for several reasons:

- Running head down, as if trying to emulate Roger Bannister, will get you lost, as you are likely to miss key junctions. This is trail running and while challenging, it is also supposed to be enjoyable. A more leisurely pace allows you to take in the views.

- The terrain is not uniform and consistent underfoot. This will not only slow you down, but also challenge other proprioceptive muscles which will fatigue you much sooner.

- The gradient off-road is much steeper on the ups and downs. Some of the routes in this book involve uphill sections which most of us are unable to run up, and some of the downhills can only be attempted at speed if you are well practised in this skill. Most running club sessions include hill sessions, but only ever uphill. Downhill training is often neglected.

- The cadence is much higher on trails and fells, and constantly changes which breaks your rhythm, making it more difficult to get into your stride and pace.

Considering the above, it begs the question: why would you want to run on trails and fells in the first place? Because it is much more fun! Give me a jaunt around the trails and fells of Dartmoor any day over the petrol-fumed roadside pavements of a town or city.

There are other aspects which can benefit the avid road runner in the long run. Leg strength is one such bonus, as is a better core and balance from which to power your road running 10k personal best. The repetitive pounding of the tarmac can also cause muscle imbalances and overuse injuries, which can potentially be prevented by incorporating running on a different surface such as a trail or the fells.

Yet the benefits are not just physical. Running in the natural environment is generally accepted to be beneficial for mental health. Just look at any Instagram feed associated with running, or any running shoe marketing campaign and the backdrop will inevitably be one of beautiful, natural surroundings. Dartmoor is a very spiritual place, and its natural environment is used by many mental health charities as

How to Use this Guide

Checkpoint at Shipley Bridge

their classroom. Ironically, the charities associated with treating service personnel for mental health issues such as PTSD, use the same training area that, the powers-that-be, used to make them into a soldier in the first place.

The routes in this guide will enable both the fast, competitive runner and the recreational jogger to run on some of the best trails and fells Dartmoor National Park has to offer, and benefit each one both physically and mentally.

The routes are split into two categories: trail (T) and fell (F) and there is a difference between the two.

Trail running can be described as running on obvious paths and tracks, often signposted. The surface is usually well-defined and not too technical (see below for grading and classification of routes). For those new to running off-road, this is an ideal place to start, and I would advise running a few trail routes prior to some of the fell runs described in this book.

Fell running or hill running differs slightly from trail, in that many of the paths are less defined, if there at all. Also, the gradients are often much steeper and the surface much more difficult underfoot. These routes will involve some running off the beaten track, so be warned.

There is an argument, not supported by me, that fell running is a predominantly northern sport. Indeed, the North West in particular is the unofficial home of British fell running, but while Dartmoor doesn't necessarily have the altitude, it definitely has the terrain.

Classification of routes

Please note; this is my own grading system and not an official method. There are gradings for the trail race circuit and the Fell Running Association (FRA) have their own classification based on distance and ascent.

How to Use this Guide

Weather on Dartmoor is unpredictable. – MBa

However, I have tried to simplify this purely for the purpose of the routes contained in this book and for Dartmoor National Park. I have also not included height in the classification because, as a rule, these routes are going to involve more uphill than most road runs and generally involve a healthy amount of ascent and descent as per the terrain.

The degree of technical terrain relates to how smooth the path is underfoot. The higher the grade, the more technical or rough the terrain is underfoot.

> T1a: Short distance, less than 5 miles with no technical terrain
> T1b: Short distance, less than 5 miles with some technical terrain
> T2a: Medium distance, 5-10 miles with no technical terrain
> T2b: Medium distance, 5-10 miles with some technical terrain
> T3a: Long distance, 10 miles plus with no technical terrain
> T3b: Long distance, 10 miles plus with some technical terrain
> F1: Short distance, less than 5 miles
> F2: Medium distance, 5-10 miles
> F3: Long distance, 10 miles plus
> (Fell running routes by their nature involve a degree of technicality).

Running Safely on Dartmoor

In addition to all the recreational activities that take place in the park, the land is still a place of work and a source of income for many. Beef, dairy, and sheep farming are still abundant on Dartmoor, and due to its open moorland nature, these beasts roam freely across the roads and lanes. Sadly, livestock are lost all too frequently to road collisions, due mainly to vehicles travelling too fast, only to suddenly discover an animal in the middle of the road. Dartmoor ponies, an iconic sight across all corners of the moor, also have particularly poor Green Cross Code skills, and unfortunately congregate close to roadsides in the search for discarded food. Bottom line is, *"take moor care"* (Dartmoor National Park Authority) when driving across the moor.

Live firing ranges

The Ministry of Defence also have three, live firing ranges on the north moor: Okehampton, Willsworthy, and Merrivale. Live firing can take place at any time of year, day and night within these ranges and they are out of bounds at these times. However, they are very rarely used at weekends and not every day of the week. Use the link below to find out in advance when and where firing takes place. The ranges are patrolled by wardens, marked by permanent red and white range markers, and temporary red flags on the surrounding tors. Entering the ranges during firing not only causes major military exercises to cease, it also potentially causes loss of life on both sides and risks a run-in with the law.

To find out which ranges are in use and when, go to the website: www.gov.uk/government/publications/dartmoor-firing-programme.

Each route in this book will inform you if it enters the firing ranges at any point.

In addition to the live firing in these areas, the military does train frequently on other areas of the moor, but only with blank ammunition and then only under certain circumstances.

On any part of Dartmoor, it is not unusual to come across used ammunition ordnance such as smoke grenades etc. While I can assure you that every effort to remove such items is taken, mistakes do happen, and some do get left out on the moor. It is imperative that none of these items are touched just in case of a partial detonation or that the item may still be live. Touching or carrying the item off the training area potentially risks injury and / or death. For more information on this, go to: www.dartmoor.gov.uk/living-and-working/access-and-land-management/military-on-dartmoor.

Range warning sign

Running Safely on Dartmoor

Weather conditions and climate

'Climate' is the term used to describe long-term weather patterns, and Devon's is much like the rest of the temperate climate associated with the United Kingdom, which is influenced by the Atlantic Ocean to the west. However, being situated in the South West and the prevailing weather coming from that direction, Devon tends to catch it first, whether it be fine or wet conditions. So, as a rule of thumb we can probably safely say that the area's south-westerly position makes it generally warmer, yet wetter and windier, than most other parts of the country.

Dartmoor, however, adds a couple of extra factors into the mix. The higher altitude and exposed landscape makes the weather here a little more extreme. There is a general pattern where the higher the relief (altitude), the greater the likelihood of precipitation. Once the damp air is blown up over the granite mass of Dartmoor from the south-west, it cools, producing clouds and inevitably precipitation.

One of the key indicators of the climate on Dartmoor is the distinct lack of trees. Those that remain, such as the dwarf oak trees at Wistman's Wood, and the lone, gnarled tree on the summit of Sharp Tor, are all twisted and bent out of shape. Another, is the fact that there are eight reservoirs located on the moor, providing the South West with one of its most important sources of water. These don't fill by themselves and, according to the Dartmoor National Park Authority, Princetown, in the rough centre of the moor, receives, on average, twice the annual rainfall compared to towns on the south coast of Devon.

The temperature is frequently 2 to 4 degrees lower at the top of North Hessary Tor, at 510 metres above sea level, than lowland woodland on the eastern side of the moor, at less than 200 metres above sea level. A common weather condition of Dartmoor is blanket fog, which rolls over from the south-west making the temperature drop and visibility challenging. In fact, the moor is famous for it. Sir Arthur Conan Doyle based his suspense on the fog in which the Hound of the Baskervilles hid, in his book of the same name:

"In all England there is no district more dismal than the vast expanse of primitive wasteland, the moors of Dartmoor in Devonshire".

So, what does this means for us, the off-road runner on Dartmoor?

Check the conditions prior to setting off and match this with your experience and ability. If the weather is bad and you consider yourself a novice with limited local knowledge, then choose a different place to run. Within the route descriptions of this book, I have made it clear which routes to be wary of in bad weather. Dress or carry the right kit for the job. The weather can change in an instant and in a 5-mile run on the tops of Dartmoor I have gone from running in blue skies to full on blanket fog and mizzle. You have been warned. Read the chapter on clothing and equipment to get the guidance and knowledge.

Dartmoor should be classed as a British, mountainous area when it comes to weather conditions, and in particular navigation. There is a saying among outdoor types in the know, which states that, if you can navigate on Dartmoor, you can navigate anywhere. This is due to the lack of key features such as large mountain tops, huge rivers, or a plethora of villages and roads. Please do not underestimate it.

The Countryside Code

This is largely accepted as the rules governing visitors behaviour (including runners) when it comes to using the countryside as a recreational space, and as such, should be adhered to by all. Here is a summary, as per the government guidance, with a few additions from myself.

- Respect everyone.

- Be considerate to those living in, working in, and enjoying the countryside.

- Leave gates and property as you find them; so if gates are closed, close them again.

- Do not block access to gateways or driveways when parking.

- Be nice, say *'hello'*, share the space. Often runners get a bad reputation for head-down ignorance. If coming up on a narrow path behind a walker then call out *'excuse me'* in good time and say *'thank you'* as you pass.

- Follow local signs and keep to marked paths unless wider access is available. Much of Dartmoor is open access land so allows you to roam, but respect private land.

- Protect the environment and take your litter home. Leave no trace of your visit.

- Do not light fires and only have BBQs where signs say you can. Do not use disposable barbecues. They are just that, and so bad for the environment during use and certainly after.

- Always keep dogs under control and in sight. Lambing season is generally in March and April but can be either side of this so take extra care at this time.

- Bear in mind also that Dartmoor is home to birds such as the meadow pipit and stonechat, which build their nests on the ground between the 1st of March and 31st of July. These areas can be found at the following website and it is generally accepted that they be avoided where possible during nesting season: https://www.dartmoor.gov.uk/wildlife-and-heritage/wildlife/birds/birds-nesting

- Dog poo – bag it and bin it – any public waste bin will do.

- Care for nature and do not cause damage or disturbance to the natural habitat.

- Check your route and local conditions.

Well-equipped fell runners – ML

Clothing and Equipment

What to wear and how to wear it.

Many of the more experienced off-road runners will either skip this chapter completely or read it with the intention of finding a particular point to disagree with. However, this is only my advice and opinion from many years of learning from my mistakes, learning from my peers, and continually learning as fabrics and equipment develop. Every day is a school day someone once said, so while you are here, read on and you just might pick up something useful.

One of the godfathers of walking on the trails and footpaths, Alfred Wainwright wrote in his 1973 book A Coast-to-Coast Walk:

"There is no such thing as bad weather, only unsuitable clothing."

While I agree with him, I would go so far as to change it slightly to: *"and the inability to wear suitable clothing."*

In essence, all we need to wear to run is some loose clothing and maybe a pair of running shoes, or not, depending on which side of the barefoot debate you reside. The multi-million pound sportswear and equipment industry would disagree though, and judging by its ever-growing popularity so would we. Indeed, to run across the high moors of Dartmoor in just a pair of shorts and a gym shirt in most seasons would probably buy you a golden ticket to the back of a Dartmoor Rescue Land Rover.

Yet this is not a chapter designed to encourage you to unholster the loaded credit card and point it in the direction of the nearest running shop. In running, and in particular trail and fell running, less is generally more, and you would be foolish to buy everything listed in this chapter if you didn't run the lengthier distances, didn't run in poor weather, and had no intention of entering any events (which often have a minimum kit requirement so as to meet the governing body regulations, and keep you safe in the event of an emergency).

However, it would be remiss of me not to provide you with at least the bare minimum of kit required for the routes identified in this book, purely from a safety point of view.

Clothing

I started this chapter by adding an extra embellishment to Alfred Wainwrights quote and I reiterate it now; *"and the inability to wear suitable clothing"*, and I should explain this now.

Throughout my career as a Royal Marine, Mountain Leader, and running guide, I have seen people with the right clothing but not necessarily worn for the right weather, and certainly not wearing them correctly. For example, a waterproof jacket is not designed to be worn continuously on a showery summer's day for a four mile run, and the chances are the wearer will get wetter from perspiration than precipitation.

Hypothermia is a real risk all year-round when out on the trails or fells. By its very nature, running off-road takes us into a different environment, away from the relative comfort of towns, and out into less densely populated areas. The weather is an obvious factor in this, but in general, when running, the body's

Clothing and Equipment

temperature is at a comfortable level in cold conditions. However, when we stop, our body temperature reduces quickly, with the assistance of wind, precipitation, altitude and air temperature.

Having to stop is sometimes unavoidable, for example if we twist an ankle, or worse. With no activity to keep us warm, the only protection is from our clothing and gear that we wear or carry. Being left out on the open moor until help arrives, even in the summer months, can cause the body temperature to drop to dangerous levels, and this is when hypothermia can occur, causing a genuine threat to life.

So, before we look at the ranges of clothing, the options available and their limitations as well as when and how it should be worn, remember to wear and / or carry clothing appropriate for the worst case scenario.

Base layer

Let us start with the layer next to the body or skin. The material should be light and of a technical nature rather than cotton. Others might call this wicking material. There are a wide range of options available and with different features, from thumb loops to rear pockets to stash your goodies. The budgets vary as per the brand name and quality. Merino wool, while ace at regulating temperature, can be expensive and too warm in hot conditions.

Personally, I prefer a long sleeve as opposed to short, even on warmer days due to its flexibility when out on the trail. If I am running around a town, at speed, then generally a short sleeve is fine as the town can offer more shelter, and shops, cafés etc. to rush into if a mini ice age should catch you out. Out on the hills, fells, or trails though, shelter is less abundant, as are people willing to take you in and / or call for assistance if needed.

A long sleeve not only provides warmth in the cool but can also keep the skin covered in bright, hot sunshine to prevent burning, sleeves can be rolled up to act like a short sleeve, and more importantly are essential if wearing a waterproof. More on this later.

On the bottom half, shorts or leggings / tights can be worn, the latter providing more warmth, and protection from gorse bushes, rocks and sheep / deer ticks. Personally, I'm a shorts man generally, as I find tights get heavy in the wet, but this is personal preference and the pros and cons of either are obvious. However, many winter fell and trail events require full leg cover, or at least stipulate that they are carried in case of emergency.

Dartmoor, not unlike many other areas in Europe is an area that is blighted by ticks. Ticks can carry Lyme disease and so they are far from desirable. If running through long grass, full leg cover can be useful for prevention of ticks, or a ¾ capri-type garment, coupled with calf length socks.

Note: There are many theories about how to deal with ticks from Vaseline to a lit match. However, the safest way, in my experience, is to get a plastic tick remover and deal with it as soon as possible. Get your buddies or someone more personal to you, to check the areas of your body that you can't see on return from your run. Ticks like warm areas such as the back of knees or the groin area, and they crawl!

If you fail to discover one, and after a while experience a bullseye-type ring where a tick may have got hold of you, or flu-like symptoms develop, seek medical attention. Ticks can transmit Lyme disease which is a potentially serious illness, but which can be easily dealt with if treated with antibiotics at an early stage.

Clothing and Equipment

When out running, stay in tune with your body. If you feel hot, lose a layer. If you feel cold while running, put on an extra layer sooner rather than later, and before it's too late.

My race partner on the Three Peaks Yacht Race, when climbing the final peak, Ben Nevis, in July, failed to layer-up soon enough as we climbed. We were not moving particularly fast, and the driving snow hampered our speed. With the wind chill factored in, the temperature was well below freezing. Eventually after much cajoling, I persuaded her to stop and add an extra layer, hat, and gloves. By this time, it was a little too late, and it took both of us ten minutes or more to get her dressed. By which time, her core body temperature had fallen to dangerous levels. The steep climb and loads of chocolate warmed her sufficiently to carry on, but this, after four days of racing, could have been the end of our race and, even more dramatically, her life.

Waterproofs vs windproof

First, let me begin by saying, no waterproof will keep you completely dry. Yes, the fabric might be 100% waterproof, but a jacket still has holes for the head and hands etc. and water will find its way in somehow. However, a waterproof jacket will keep most of the wet, and also the wind, out, preventing the body from cooling. A windproof does just what it says, and keeps the wind off but not the rain. The question is, do you need to carry or wear one?

Let us start at worst-case scenario and work back to get a clearer picture. If we are doing many of the trail and fell races in this country and abroad, the chances are a waterproof jacket with taped seams is an essential part of the kit list, and without which you cannot enter. Should they do a kit check that is.

It could be that you end up just carrying it in your pack or bum bag, but as explained earlier, conditions change, and you might have to stop.

Windproof – Inov-8

Waterproof with taped seams – Inov-8

Clothing and Equipment

There are a wide selection of options and brands out there and, in general, the greater the cost, the better the jacket. However, if you are not straying far on your runs, race infrequently and are a fair-weather runner, you probably don't need to buy the most expensive one you can find.

When choosing one, by all means read the reviews, but these are often very subjective and many runners are brand loyal. Better still, get into a store and try some on. Each brand and model fit differently with different body shapes, sleeve lengths and sizes. A size 14 in one brand could be a 12 in another.

Once you have got one on, zip it all the way up to the chin, and into the zip guard. Not doing up a zip on a waterproof jacket is like not putting a lid on a blender. Make sure it's comfortable but most importantly is not too big! This is one of my pet dislikes. Guaranteed – a waterproof jacket that is too big will get the runner wet on a run.

To substantiate my statement let me explain how a jacket that is supposedly 100% waterproof, can let water vapour out. Rainwater falls on to a jacket and should bead off. This happens better if there is perspiration, or evaporated moisture, pushing out from the inside, provided by the runner. As the runner moves, the heat generated and subsequent perspiration, sweat to some of us, is forced out through the micropores of the jacket, keeping the garment dry.

If, however, the garment doesn't fit close to the body, the perspiration comes off the body and, instead of being forced out, cools rapidly and condenses, or turns into droplets, which wet the clothing and skin. In the case of most people who claim their jacket leaks, it is either because they have not zipped it up properly, have bought one that is too big, or have been wearing it running at full-speed in a minor drizzle. Just as with tent material, if skin comes into contact with it, the garment will potentially leak, which is the reason why long sleeves work best as base layers.

Please bear in mind that if you intend to wear a pack over the top, then breathability of the garment is hindered for obvious reasons. Expect to get damp over the shoulders and back where the pack is in contact with your body..

You don't need to test a waterproof jacket by putting your arms up in the air to see if it rides up. No one runs like this, except maybe as you cross the finish line in first place. Exactly. Your arms should move freely, and the hood should cover the whole head.

Just to confirm what 'taped seams' are; look inside a waterproof jacket and look at the stitched joins on the seams. A clear tape should cover all of these to minimise leakage.

Most waterproof, running jackets have a full zip which, in my opinion, makes it more flexible. A smock type jacket may be lighter and more waterproof due to the lack of full-length zip but are more difficult to put on and take off. Again, my recommendation is to go into a store, with specialist running staff, and try some on to see what works for you.

As previously mentioned, a waterproof jacket can help keep you safe in the event of an emergency on the trails, and if heading out for a long run over exposed and remote landscapes, I would always carry one. However, if I am going out for a short, fast run and the forecast is for light rain, I might just take a windproof.

Windproofs are lighter and in general, for most recreational runners, are more than sufficient. They are cheaper too.

Clothing and Equipment

These garments should fit like a waterproof, but often don't have a hood. They breathe better than a waterproof and are just designed to keep the windchill factor off. If it rains, you will get wet, but it's the wind that makes you cold. I personally wear a windproof through most of the winter months while running across the moor and carry a waterproof. It means I do not perspire as much and it extends the life of my expensive waterproof jacket, as I rarely use it.

Hats and gloves

Approximately 70 percent of heat is lost through the head (British Mountaineering Council), so a hat is always on the kit list of fell and trail races, and always in my bumbag or pack. I find that if my hands are cold, the donning of a hat keeps them warmer as less heat is escaping from my body. A cap in cold weather is no substitute for a warm beanie. There are lots out there, just go with what works or suits you.

Mitts are warmer than gloves – Inov-8

As for gloves, while the traditional glove aids dexterity when using tech gadgets, they are not as good at keeping the hands warm in very cold conditions. This is generally because each digit does not generate much heat on its own, due to a poor blood supply. Also, the greater surface area of a glove means more heat is lost. Conversely, a mitt keeps all the fingers and hand in one area, sharing body heat. Look at Arctic explorers and check out their hands. All wear mitts and not gloves. Many UK climates do not get that cold, but if you know that you suffer from cold hands for whatever reason, consider a mitt rather than a glove. We are running after all, not climbing, or typing.

Socks

Wow, for something as simple as a covering for the humble foot, who would have thought that there could be so many different options? There are waterproof socks, toe socks, merino, infra-red, mohair, quarter length, ankle, crew, no-show, compression ... the list goes on.

This is such a personal thing; it would be wrong of me to recommend a certain type or brand:
"The book said I should get these socks, yet I got huge blisters and came last in a race ... "
Just try a selection and go with what works for you. What I would say is that on fells and trail, avoid no-show socks, ones that you can't see and only just cover the foot. Debris from the trail can get in the shoe more easily, and you are more likely to get ankle scratches than with a higher, ankle sock. Just my opinion from years of experience. Higher socks may look more like what your grandad wore, but look better than scabby ankles when wearing your heels or sandals.

Clothing and Equipment

Equipment

As well as clothing, there are more items to spend your money on. Some being desirable and others, you might say, are essential. Here we look at some of the options.

To pole or not to pole
Running poles have become more popular in the last twenty years or so, although more so on the continent than over here in the United Kingdom.
On long events such as ultras of over 50 miles, they can be extremely useful, depending on the terrain. I had never used them prior to my UTMB, and borrowed a pair solely for the purpose of this event. My previous fell events and British ultras either forbade their use or they just were not suitable. Poles on soft ground are not an asset, believe me. However, I failed to practice with the poles and only started to feel the benefit of them for the last few miles, by which time my arms were more trashed than my legs.
To that end, if you do intend to use poles and think they may be useful, be sure to get some instruction and practice well in advance.
For the routes in this book, I very much doubt that poles would be required, other than on the north to south crossing.

Safety bits and pieces
Most events now require a whistle, first aid kit and an emergency blanket, and for good reason. Personally, on a long, remote run, I would take an emergency bivvy bag or similar. A phone could also be useful.

Running pack or waist bag
In general, the further you run, the more safety kit you will probably want to carry, so go for a pack rather than a bumbag. Bumbags can carry mandatory Fell Running Association (FRA) kit, but, if inexperienced I would recommend taking more.

Bumbag for essentials – Inov-8   Running vest or pack – Inov-8

Clothing and Equipment

Some folk love a hydration system, involving a bladder and tube, over a soft flask or bottle system in the front. I prefer a front, soft flask system for ease of refilling, and regulation of hydration, i.e., it's easier to see how much you have drunk or have got left over a bladder. Soft flasks are easier to clean too.

Again, it is not for me to recommend one or the other when it comes to brands, just go into a physical store, try some on and, if necessary, get fitted properly.

When it comes to size of packs, or capacity, there are a couple of things to bear in mind. If you never intend to run more than a few miles, up to ten say, then all you need is 3 to 5 litres capacity. Most bumbags are 3 litres and are sufficient. However, if you are on the slower side and likely to be out for longer, then probably carry more in the way of food, fluids and clothes. So maybe a 5-litre pack would be better.

If you are considering racing at the front end of races, then go smaller, as weight obviously matters. Just ensure you have enough space to carry the required kit.

For those on half to full-day excursions or longer, then I would say that 10 litres is a minimum size pack to ensure all food and kit can be carried. Of course, if stopping at checkpoints or villages on the way, you might not need to carry as much but do not rely on this. Checkpoints could be poorly stocked, and shops could be closed.

If more kit is required, consider taking a 5 to 10-litre pack plus a bumbag of 3 litres. This gives greater flexibility and is more cost effective than buying a different pack for all eventualities.

Note: at this point I should mention that I wouldn't recommend drinking from water sources on Dartmoor without sterilizing. Unlike the mountains of Scotland for example, the moors are relatively low-lying and sheep roam everywhere.

Footwear

I purposefully left this until last as this is always a hot topic, particularly more recently with a model of shoe for every surface. Back in the day, you had road shoes or a studded shoe, or boot. Advice for what shoe one should wear for this race, or that surface is free online, and in print, with everyone having an opinion. *"My hairdresser says that this shoe is great as they wear them, so I would like the same too."* is a phrase I have heard not once but three times in store.

To that end, I am not going to tell you what shoe to wear, as like our feet, each shoe, model, and brand are different. I obviously have my own opinions on what I think works best and, thanks to experience, I believe I can make an informed decision, but it is still only an opinion. However, there are a few things to take into consideration when choosing a running shoe. After all, this is perhaps the most important part of your running equipment.

- Go into an independent running store. These are normally owned and operated by runners of all standards and abilities and can offer you the best advice. Not only that, but you should also be able to try on a wide range of shoes for your chosen surface and running style. Trying the actual shoe on is far better than reading or watching numerous reviews or taking recommendations from your hair stylist!

Clothing and Equipment

Trail shoe

- Try lots of shoes on. Every brand sizes differently, have different last widths and shape.

- In general, a road shoe has a flat outsole, to give as much contact with the ground as possible for better grip, and a light, soft upper for comfort and speed. A trail shoe has a more robust upper to deal with rougher terrain, and in general a more aggressive outsole to grip on rocky and uneven terrain. A fell shoe tends to be closer to the ground for a better feel of the ground, for balance purposes, and a series of rubber studs to sink into the mud and grass. Conversely, these are less appropriate for the road as there is a lack of contact with the ground, and the studs will degrade quicker.

To that end, you should choose the most appropriate shoe for the majority of the surfaces you are going to run on, your own ability, running style and the level of comfort that you are used to.

For example, I prefer a studded shoe on most off-road surfaces as it is what I feel comfortable in, can trust on all surfaces and I like to feel the ground, like a ballet dancer … I wish!

I am also relatively quicker on fells than I am on road. To that end I play to my strengths and use a shoe with lots of grip to maximise my skill and advantage. In the USA they would call this a power-play.

- Reviews are useful, but the reviewer has not got the same feet or running style as you.

- Rotate your shoes. It is false economy to have one pair of shoes that you use for everything. By having two or three pairs of different types, the shoes will last longer. For example, as a massive running shoe geek, I have a shoe for all occasions. I have a pair of

Clothing and Equipment

Fell shoe (more agressive sole)

racing fell shoes, a pair of training fell shoes (both studded and low profile to feel the ground), a pair of racing trail shoes, a pair of training trail shoes, a pair of hybrid road to trail, a pair of road racing shoes and a pair of road training shoes. Hey, it is my sport and all together those shoes are still cheaper than your average bike.

- Cost. It is what it is, running shoes are expensive and if, like me, you run anything from 20-50 miles a week, it won't be long before they need replacing. However, the expense is relative compared to a new bike which requires a service, new tyres, brakes etc. The average ladies' haircut is more than half the price of a new pair of shoes, so suck it up or choose to run barefoot, or choose another sport.

Waterproof or not waterproof?
My advice is to avoid waterproof running shoes for a number of reasons.
Firstly, a waterproof running shoe is only as waterproof as it is high. If water goes over the top of the shoe, water will not only get in, but it won't get out either. Wet feet for the remainder of the run. On the routes in this book, there is a definite risk of water going over the top of the shoe. You want water to get out quickly if it gets in. A boot is different, as it is higher.
Secondly, feet sweat, and you are just as likely to get wet feet from perspiration, as you are water from outside.
Thirdly, the waterproof membrane makes the shoe more expensive, more likely to fail over time, and a snugger fit due to the membrane. Size up if you must choose a waterproof running shoe.
Waterproof shoes are great for dog walks or commuting to work, but for trail and fell running get used to wet feet. You could consider waterproof socks, but again, perspiration is an issue unless it is very cold.

Running on Dartmoor – ML

North West

Dartmoor National Park has so many different characteristics and this is defined primarily by Mother Nature. The relief, rivers, vegetation and relative occurrence of all of the above strive to carve a different personality for each region, and the human settlements, old and new, have only added to this.

The North West can be easily described as the wild and rugged quarter of the moor, with its high tors and steep valleys. The prevailing westerlies mean this side bears the brunt of any bad weather. Indeed, in 1644 after King Charles I visited the town of Tavistock on the western edge of the moor, when asked about the weather in England he said:

"if it is raining anywhere in my kingdom it will be raining in Tavistock."

The main towns from which to plan these excursions from are Okehampton on the northern tip of the moor, and Tavistock over to the west, just outside the national park boundary.

Arms Tor - SW

Langstone menhir (just off Route 5) – SW

Meldon Reservoir Loop 1

Meldon Reservoir

1 Meldon Reservoir Loop

Distance	7.2km (4.5 miles)
Ascent	194m (635ft)
Grade	T1a
Start / Finish	Meldon Reservoir car park SX 562 917 (50.7078 -4.0386)

This route is an easy one to follow, does not take long and does not enter the firing range. It is perfect as a stress reliever where all you want to do is run, without concentrating too much. I have used this run as a mid-commute break while driving on the main A30. Looking up at the moor from my car, the last place I want to be is on the road, but when short of time, I can't venture off too far or for too long, this quick fix is perfect.

It's also a great run for those new to the moor and who want to experience the national park, without going too far off the beaten track. The route follows paths and tracks and has the navigational advantage of having a large reservoir as the centre piece.

Meldon Reservoir has a roomy car park to start from and is administered by the National Park and, just as important, has a loo. There is a charge of £1 for three hours which is enough for those running without picnic or swim stops. There is no café, however, there is a service station just off the main A30 five minutes drive away, and the town of Okehampton is only 3 miles to the north. That said, the banks of the reservoir are an ideal spot to munch a sandwich or two after this run as the views are stunning.

1 Meldon Reservoir Loop

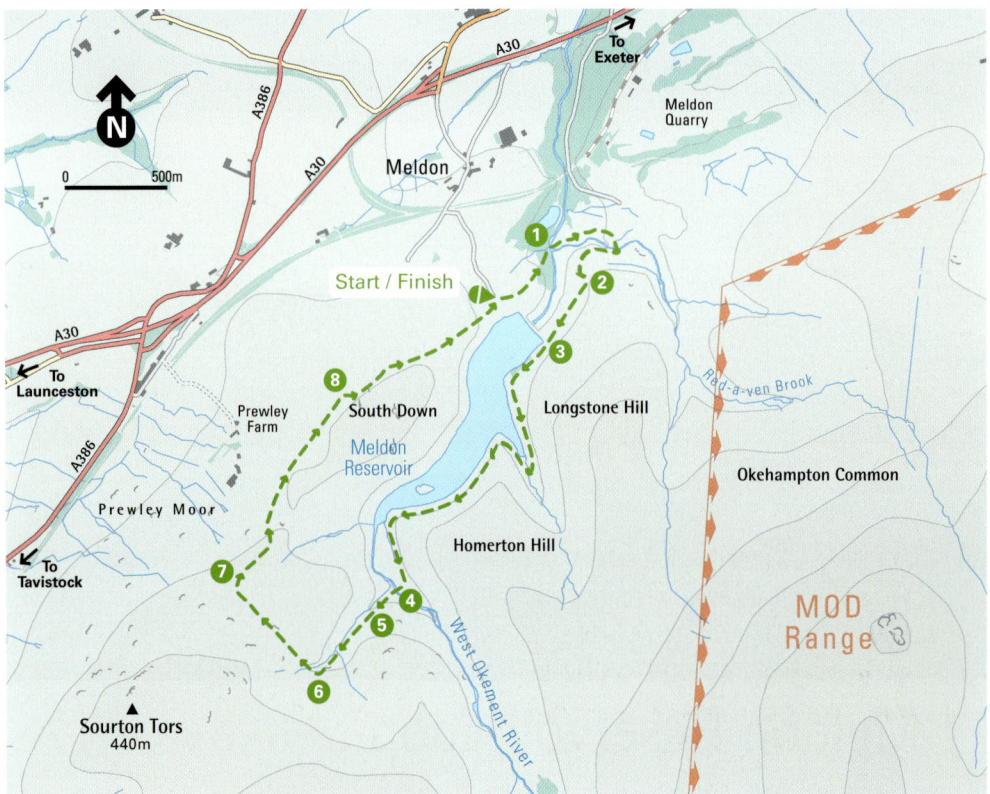

This route can be run either clockwise or anticlockwise, but I have chosen this particular way so as to finish on a downhill, as per a request from my wife who insists this finishes the run with a smile.

Route

Turn left out of the car park and follow the river downstream to a bridge. Cross, and turn right to ascend the other side of the valley along paths and tracks to run a clockwise circuit of the reservoir.

Detailed directions

START From the car park climb the steps by the loo and turn left on the lane at the top. Turn immediately left through a gate and descend a broad gravel track. Bear right at the open field to access a footbridge on the right at the bottom opposite a large pool.

❶ Cross over, and follow the track as it bends right then left up to some old quarry buildings. Turn right in front of one large building to cross a river and follow the track around to the right of the old quarry. The path now bears left and starts to climb steadily with the view of the dam dead ahead.

❷ Take the right fork on a thin path (not shown on the OS map) and after a while the gradient eases. The path heads straight up to the left-hand edge of the dam and meets a gate. Go through and head straight on. Do not cross the dam.

Meldon Reservoir Loop 1

Meldon Reservoir with Black Tor in the distance

❸ Follow the flat track, past a picnic area on the right by the banks of the waterside, and as the path bends left, ignore the sharp left track going back on yourself, go straight on following the public footpath sign. The path handrails the side of the reservoir, and then turns sharp right to cross a footbridge by some trees. Follow the path up, right and then left, around the perimeter.

❹ The going is good here, if slightly uphill before meeting the upper southern edges of the reservoir by some open marshland. The first bridge on the right is closed, so follow the inlet of the West Okement River to a concrete weir, and cross here.

Meldon dam

❺ Once across, turn right and follow the path up. The path then turns steep left up a re-entrant or valley on the streams left-hand side – keep on this to the top. A sign on the other side says no access so this is the only way around.

❻ At the top, the path typically seems to disappear due to the ever-changing wet boggy terrain. However, bear right to cross the stream by a wall corner, and pick up the path again. The path follows the line of the wall on the right, so follow this as it continues along a dry, flat portion of moorland. At the corner, turn right and follow the path to a gate.

West Devon Way

❼ Go through the gate, now on the West Devon Way, and follow this broad track sandwiched between two

Rough Dartmoor wall

Meldon Reservoir Loop

Homerton Hill

walls. Just before a gate, the path forks although this is not obvious. Follow the wall round to the right, slightly uphill, to pick up the right fork which handrails the wall on the left. The path then descends along a thin line of trees and the reservoir again comes into view on the right.

❽ Follow down to a gate, cross the lane and head back into the car park.

Heading to High Willhays

2 The Roof of Devon

Distance	12.8km (8 miles)
Ascent	403m (1,323ft)
Grade	F2
Start / Finish	Meldon Reservoir car park SX 562 917 (50.7078 -4.0386)

First and foremost, please check firing times on Okehampton Range before undertaking this run, as the route enters this particular range. The website and phone number are included earlier in this book.

Once you are all clear, you will find this route ideal for those who want to tick off a few peaks as this route climbs to the highest point on Dartmoor. According to a well-known search engine, the highest peak in southern England is only 297m high and located in the South East, at a place called Walbury Hill. I beg to differ, as at a lofty 621m above sea level, High Willhays in South West England is the highest peak in the United Kingdom, south of the Brecon Beacons.

Fortunately, the route starts at nearly 300 metres above sea level so is not a slog, but a very rewarding venture. Fifty percent of the route is on open moorland, and despite the area's popularity, the paths can become faint as people prefer to choose their own lines. To that end, take care to keep track of where you are at all times. If the weather is foggy and visibility is poor and you are not confident with map and compass, then perhaps choose a different route.

Meldon Reservoir is a well-maintained, spacious car park complete with loo. However, you do have to pay to park for the privilege; £1 for three hours. If visiting with family in tow, this is a great spot for the young

2 The Roof of Devon

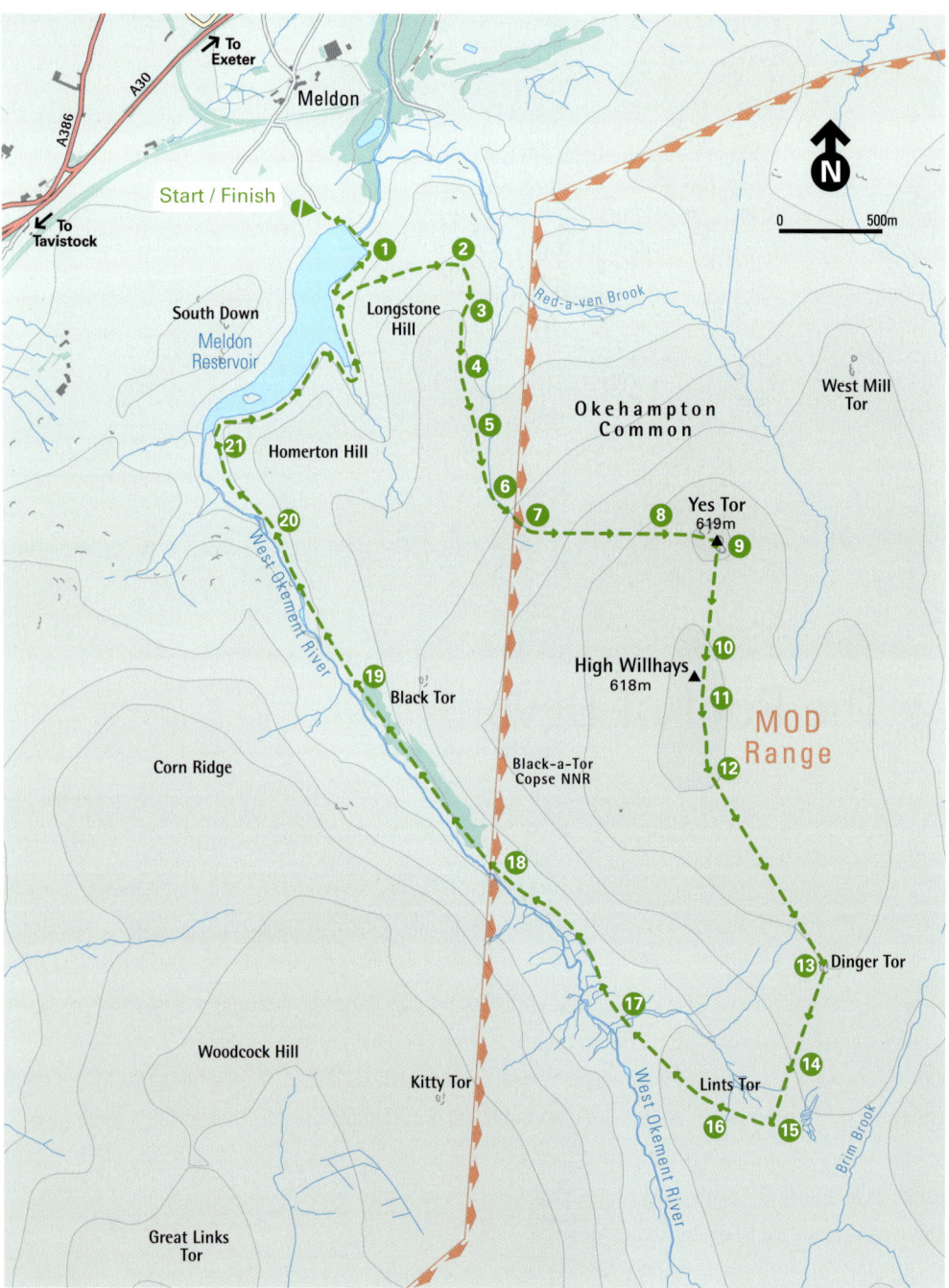

ones to explore with an adult while the other goes for their run. A short walk to the dam gives great views north over the reservoir and south over to a large viaduct showing the line of the old railway, now a cycle path called the Granite Way.

The route will visit three other tors, the upper reaches of the Okement valley and Black-a-Tor Copse, a National Nature reserve.

The Roof of Devon | 2

Route

Turn left out of the car park and cross the Meldon dam before beginning the climb to Yes Tor. From here it is an easy run south on a good track to the cairns of High Willhays. Proceed down a slight gradient and a faint but often boggy trod to Dinger Tor, before turning right to descend to Lints Tor's high stack. Follow the river downstream on the right-hand side of the valley, past the wood, and down to the reservoir and dam.

Detailed directions

START On leaving the car park, climb the steps to the right of the toilet block, pass through the gate and turn left. Follow the tarmac road down to the dam, taking in the equally stunning views both over the reservoir, and down the valley to the left.

❶ At the end of the dam, go through the metal gate and turn immediately right to follow a wide, stony track which follows the east shore of the reservoir. Follow this as the path dips and a picnic area with tables comes into view, on the right over a wooden fence. Turn sharp left here to follow the broad track uphill and almost back on yourself. Trust me, you will be glad of the gentler gradient at this point.

❷ The track starts to bend round to the right and the slope becomes gentler. Views of West Mill Tor open up ahead, weather permitting, but this is not the peak we want at this time.

❸ As the track curves further right, Yes Tor, the first peak you are aiming for comes into view, to the right of West Mill Tor. Here the track flattens and then forks. Take the left fork.

33

2 The Roof of Devon

Black-a-Tor Copse

4 After a short while, the track splits again, and again take the left option. A wooden post warns, No Cycling.

5 At the third split, still choose left and by now you will be heading straight up the slope direct to the summit of Yes Tor, although the summit is now obscured by a large boulder amongst a slope covered in clitter (a local name for the gently sloping spreads of coarse, often angular rock debris).

6 The path now becomes very faint and follows the line of a small stream. Depending on the season, this may be flowing or dry, but more than likely as is Dartmoor's want, it will just be boggy.

7 Aiming for ever straight uphill, still focusing on the boulder, you will cross into the range, signified by the red and white poles to the left and right. Useful navigational aids in thick mist.

8 Carry on for another 600m (still going uphill) to meet the boulder, picking your way carefully across the clitter, and on reaching it you will be rewarded with a view of the summit, complete with trig point on top, not 100m away, and over a very runnable gradient.

9 At the tor turn 90 degrees right and descend a path which stretches out in front along a very flat ridge. The running here is easy over a well-trodden path. Keep to the ridge making sure in bad weather not to descend either side.

10 After less than a kilometre, the rocky outcrops of the highest summit are gained, at a whole two metres higher than Yes Tor. The highest outcrop is the furthest along this track and has a finely balanced cairn on its top.

11 Feeling on top of the world, or at least the top of Dartmoor, with Yes Tor directly behind you, turn to face in a south-easterly direction and spy a low tor in the distance, just over kilometre away. This is Dinger Tor and your next feature.

The Roof of Devon 2

Black-a-Tor Copse

12 If the clag is in, a faint path leads directly to it, albeit a peaty and often soft one, encouraging many confident leaps over trainer swallowers. Still, this is very runnable and descends gently.

13 Dinger Tor is unspectacular, but is easily recognizable, due to the military hard track (the Dinger track) that comes up to meet it. The views south take in the middle of Dartmoor and some of the most remote areas such as Fur Tor and Great Kneeset.

14 Over to the right, towards the south-west, is the Okement valley and a small hill with the tall stack of Lints Tor. To run direct is shorter but foolhardy as this is rough ground littered with clitter, streams and what is known on the moor as 'elephant grass' or 'babies' heads'. So-called due to their appearance, a hard protruding head and a shot of hair sticking out the top. Its actual name, for the botanists among you, is purple moor grass (*Molina cerulea* also known as 'tussock grass'). In any case, stepping directly on top of one generally means a fall. The other indicator there is going to be some wet ground underfoot is 'bog cotton' (*Eriophorum angustifolium*), so-called because of its distinctive, cotton-wool flower head. Instead, follow the easier ground directly ahead, keeping Lints Tor to the right as you descend. The climbing is all but done for the day by this point.

15 After a couple of hundred metres, keeping Lints Tor 90 degrees to your right, you will come across a faint trod to the right, going westerly which will enable you to find your way across to its southern flank. Here you must jump a small stream, no more than a metre in width. There is a trod, as this is a popular tor, but it is easy to miss.

16 After the very short climb to the tor's base, you can now see the West Okement River below, and it is this linear feature we are to follow downstream, back to the reservoir and car park.

17 There are many trods here and the fun is in finding the best line downstream. Keeping the river on the

2 The Roof of Devon

Meldon Reservoir

left is the only requirement, but my tip is to keep to the right of the flat floodplain, where the steep flanks of High Willhays meet the valley, as this is generally more frequently used, and drier.

18 After negotiating many small streams draining into the river, you will enter Black-a-Tor Copse, and as mesmerising as it is, stay to its left, closer to the riverbank for ease of running. It is also around here that you will leave the firing range.

19 The going gets easier and at the end of the wood, Black Tor comes into view over to your right. Those that do not want to climb anymore, continue downstream, again jumping many streams to pick up a track which skirts another small, walled copse, which straddles the river.

20 The going now is easy and still downhill as the river rushes to fill the reservoir. A lush green area, popular with picnics comes into view as do a couple of footbridges over the river at the head of the reservoir. Ignore these and continue down and around to the right on the track which climbs briefly to bring in views over Meldon Reservoir.

21 Follow its east shore on a good if narrow path, as it weaves along the shore. The route swings right and descends to a footbridge over a stream coming down a steep valley, and then bears left again upon crossing, to rejoin the path around the larger body of water.

22 Reaching the dam, cross and return to the start.

The Great Links Flyer 3

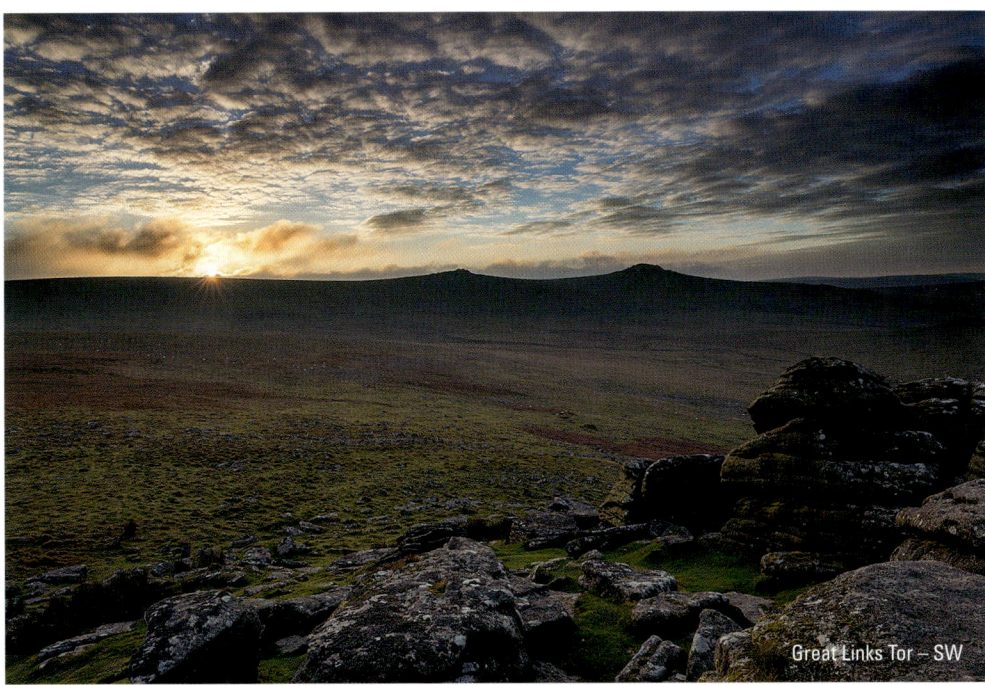

Great Links Tor – SW

3 The Great Links Flyer

Distance	8.9km (5.4 miles)
Ascent	330m (1,082ft)
Grade	F2
Start / Finish	Fox and Hounds pub SX 525 866 (50.6610 -4.0879)

This side of the moor has some great views out to the west and north, over the mass of Devon that isn't part of the National Park. However, when driving up the main road to the west of the moor it is the high tors and moorland slopes that call the keen adventurer to don a pair of running shoes and explore.

This route, while taxing, dips into the moor and its high-threatening moody character, only briefly. It therefore gives the runner the experience of the drama of the moors, while not actually venturing more than a mile into its heart. Indeed, the first hill is not even part of the same granite, igneous batholith, which dominates the National Park, and as such, has a different and friendlier feel.

The route climbs steadily for quite a while and is relentless, but not unrunnable, following the route of an old railway and military road. Those that persist are rewarded by an invigorating descent back to the start. Great Links Tor on the route is the highest point, and an outstanding example of a Dartmoor tor, quickly followed by Brat Tor with is high concrete Widgery Cross on top.

This run does not encroach on to any firing ranges, but being on the west side of the moor, can be clouded in mist and poor weather at a moment's notice. If this happens, just head west, back from where you came until you hit the road.

3 The Great Links Flyer

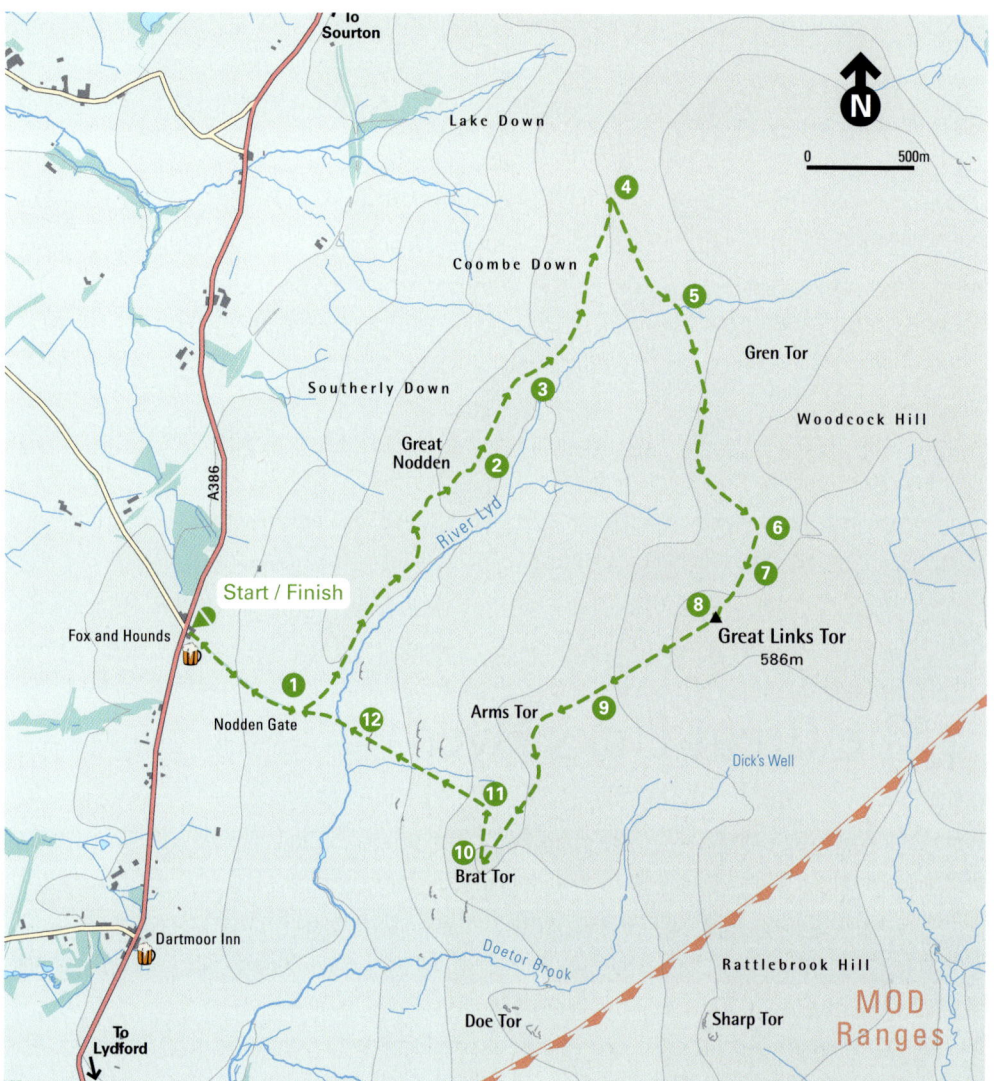

Route

From the pub car park, head up the track towards the moor. Turn left after the gate and head north on a track. Turn right at a Y-shaped junction, before turning right again and south to ascend the tor. Follow across two more tors to the south before turning back west, over the river and back down the track to the pub.

Detailed directions

START Parking at the Fox and Hounds pub, with the kind permission of the owners, take the track between the buildings heading up the slight incline away from the main road. This is a great warm up

The Great Links Flyer 3

before meeting a wooden gate. Go through the gate and stay to the right of the bunker-type feature on the left, following the wall on your right.

1 The track, an old peat railway, now swings left and the gradient steepens slightly. The ground is good and easily runnable as the rounded hillside of Great Nodden comes into view. As the track veers left slightly to enter a shallow cutting, a grass trod on the right, accessed by the steep bank, leads directly to the summit and is easy to follow as the gradient steepens. If you don't fancy the climb, stay on the old railway which lazily skirts the edge of the hill and brings you out in the same place.

2 The keen hill climbers among you will find a small cairn on the summit of Great Nodden and views over a much different landscape to the west. A view over to the right at the top, shows the highest summit on the run, Great Links Tor.

3 Descend the spur off the hill to the north on gentle ground and an obvious path, to rejoin the main old railway track. Turn right to cross a makeshift bridge over a small stream and continue as the track still climbs, albeit gently, and bears left. Numerous trods veer off the main track on both sides but ignore them and stay on the well-worn and well used surface.

4 The track, as it flattens out, ends in an upside down Y shape, and a track comes in from the right. This must have been the point where the train would reverse rather than do a three-point turn. Turn right on this track, almost back on yourself, and continue uphill with views over to the previously visited Great Nodden on the right, and the River Lyd.

5 The track drains well, with a small stream on the left and despite the uphill gradient, is not unduly taxing. The route crosses the young River Lyd, a good spot to cool off the dog in warm weather, and continues to swing left, as it approaches the northern flank of the next tor. (Note that a left-hand fork in the track after the ford marked on the OS map does not exist on the ground.)

6 The track straightens now and just before it enters a shallow cutting with peat either side, and at ninety degrees to the summit of Great Links Tor on your right, a couple of large boulders mark the point at which to leave the hard surface to the right and go bog-hopping. **Note:** if you reach a concrete line in the path (to assist drainage) only a few metres past this point, you can still turn right and join the faint track ahead.

7 The path now takes a different feel. The line is well trodden, the way obvious and straight, but depending on season, has varying degrees of softness. Either go hard and fast and leap the small brooks, hoping for good ground, or tread cautiously, picking your way over the drier sections. Either way, this is only for a short while, 150 metres or so and the ground becomes firmer as you start the climb.

8 An obvious trod leads up and right of the tor, and the trig point on the top of Great Links Tor is easily gained without too much fuss. The views, with the British weather's permission, are too fantastic to describe here.

9 From the original approach to the summit, bear right and head westerly to cross the small plateau and reach a small outcrop. A path leads west and straight over, down from this on good, fast ground heading to another lower tor, called Arms Tor. Look over to the left and south now as you descend, to see another tor which looks as if it has a cross on it. It does, and this is to be our final tor.

10 Upon reaching the granite-strewn boulders and crags of Arms Tor, turn left to follow a well-defined grass trod, which contours around to the right and over to Brat Tor, slowly losing height as you run along it.

3 The Great Links Flyer

Lyd valley from Brat Tor – SW

Climb to the top from this side to reach the large cross and spy the river below. Over to the right, upstream, is Nodden Gate, the gate you came through at the beginning and this is where you need to head for.

11 Turn right from the summit to face north, towards Arms Tor, and head to a large boulder. A few faint trods now lead down into the gully below and bearing left, letting the slope take you, cross a small stream before making your way over to the ford through low gorse bushes. Great Nodden should now be obvious over to the right ahead on the other side of the valley. Don't worry if you bear too far left, as when you hit the river, you simply turn right upstream and make for the ford.

11a In poor visiblity, just head straight down from the tor to the river and turn right to head upstream, until you reach a ford. If you come to a footbridge first, ignore it and carry on upstream for a short while until you see a ford, criss-crossed by paths.

12 Cross the low ford, and carry on uphill on a solid track, with a wall over to the left marking farm pasture. A path handrails the river on its left but ignore this and head straight on and up.

13 Upon reaching the top of the slope, the gate near the beginning of your run comes into view down the track in front, as you follow the wall on your left. Pass through the gate and down the track, back to the start.

4 Merrivale – Up Past the 'Giants Tummy'

Middle Staple at dawn – SW

4 Merrivale – Up Past the 'Giants Tummy'

Distance	8.8km (5.5 miles)
Ascent	320m (1,049ft)
Grade	F2
Start / Finish	Dartmoor Inn, Merrivale SX 548 751 (50.5583 -4.0499)

Dartmoor has a unique history, and evidence of this litters the National Park. From Bronze Age forts, to more recent activities, this area is rich in signs of human activity. One ubiquitous commodity is the very stone which forms the moor, the huge granite batholith, formed from igneous volcanic rock pushing up from under the earth's surface long ago.

Therefore, it is not surprising that small quarries popped up all over the area, supplying work for purpose built communities within a short distance of the quarry face. Merrivale Quarry is one such location, and the scar on the hillside seen from the road when travelling from Princetown towards Tavistock is unmissable. My youngest daughter, not fully understanding why someone would purposefully dig a big hole in the ground and then leave it, decided that it was much more likely to be the tummy of a huge giant which lay sleeping on his back. She was five at the time and an impatient yet sympathetic 'yes dear, perhaps' was much more of an agreeable conclusion than a whole explanation of human industrial heritage.

Giants notwithstanding, this route is free of all quarrying, does not cross into any of the firing ranges, and has a great, newly refurbished inn and outdoor café to start from.

4 Merrivale – Up Past the 'Giants Tummy'

The Dartmoor Inn at Merrivale (there is another on the western fringes of the moor) has great food, beer, and hot beverages to make it the perfect spot to start and finish a run, whatever the season. Parking along the lane outside and beyond the inn is off the main road and free, although it is considered good form to partake of the fare on offer as justification for parking there. Dogs, geese and random other animals are not unusual here as the farm next door is still operational.

The tone of the route itself is set by the start. Sat outside the pub, in the valley of the River Walkham, the only way is up, and not as Yazz and the Plastic People Population meant either! There is a stiff climb right from the start, but there are only two more of, what I would call 'real climbs', on the rest of the route. As a caveat, there are two fantastically fast descents, ones which cause individuals to whoop out loud as they crash down the hillsides.

All the route is runnable, depending on fitness level of course, and is easy to follow on faint, grassy Dartmoor trods. Look out on the last climb for a well-marked, paved path, known as the quarryman's path, making the walk from the settlement of Peter Tavy to the quarry an easier commute.

Merrivale – Up Past the 'Giants Tummy'   4

Route

Turn right out of the pub and head up past the quarry to the top of the ridge. Turn right and head NNE across the tors and out across the moor. Turn left and head NW to cross a river and ascend White Tor. Return downhill in a southerly direction to the river and up between Cox Tor and Great Staple Tor before turning left and heading SE over the ridge, finally descending back to the start.

Detailed directions

Great Mis Tor from White Hill – SW

START Facing the road outside the Inn, turn right up the grassy verge to a clearing before a stone cottage. Turn right here, over the tussocks between a wall on the right and the rocky spoils of the quarry on the left. The clearing narrows to cross broken ground over a stream, and once over the stream and into a wider clearing, bear left to follow the line of the stream and quarry deposits on the left. An obvious trod marks this for you.

❶ The route now comes on to a hard standing with a farm track running left to right, and the first steep climb straight ahead. Cross the track and head up the slope, keeping initially slightly right, by the small brook. This is to ensure a good crossing over the leat ahead via a stone bridge. After the bridge the faint trod swings left but still climbing, and then right to go directly up. In any case, just head up the slope. If you head too far left, you hit a fence guarding the quarry or 'giants tummy'. In this case, just continue uphill to gain the ridge.

❷ The trod and / or slope eventually level off at a saddle between two tors. An obvious crossroads in the grass trod marks the spot where you turn right to head up to the first of three tors on the route. This is Great Staple Tor. Pass through the middle of the rocky outcrop, before heading straight along down to a boundary stone and up to the top of the next one; Roos Tor. The running is easy and views are outstanding in fine weather.

❸ After the second tor, the grassy reaches in front have a path either side. In this instance, take the right path which descends gently with the River Walkham on the right, and Great Mis Tor high up above the valley side. Follow the wide, soft path which is excellent to run along for quite a while. It just starts to level out and climb gently where a small pile of stones marks the point of a left turn. Your back stop, or point where you have gone too far is the red and white range poles just a short distance ahead. If you reach these, you have gone too far.

❹ Turn left at the stones to spy another grassy trod, frequently used by quad bikes, and follow as it rises gently over the hill. The triangular shape of White Tor comes into view ahead, and is the general direction

4 Merrivale – Up Past the 'Giants Tummy'

of the route. Eventually the path comes out at a wall corner by a stone track. Turn right here on the track to cross through a ford. If you hit the wall early, turn right until you reach the corner.

❺ Once through the ford, follow the track uphill to another track running left to right. Cross over, and head for the right hand side of the tor ahead. The path is now hard to follow as the ground turns into hundreds of small grassy moguls. Approaching the rocky outcrop on the right, a stone range hut is obvious by its square shape. Head for this and just in front, turn left to follow the thin path over the low walls of the Bronze age boundary wall heading for the flag pole in the centre of White Tor.

❻ At the flagpole, turn left to face a big boulder and follow the path just off to the left of it, descending down the hillside. This faint path turns

White Tor – SW

into a larger path, which swings right to join the same military track crossed earlier. Cross over and follow the obvious raised long mound, or BUND line in military terms (Built Up Natural Defence), down the grassy slope.

❼ Head down to the corner of a wall, across a stream. Do this by heading straight down, and hitting the stream, then just turn right until you reach the ford by a gate. Cross the stream, and through the gate. Turn half-right, following the small public footpath sign and cross the pasture land on an obvious path to another gate, which opens on to open moorland. Follow the path right after going through the gate, until it meets a tree by a wall corner. At this point, turn left to climb up a slope which looks like a shallow valley between Great Staple Tor and Cox Tor. There is a path but it is very faint and often lost. Stay in the middle and climb up to the dip on the horizon. A key marker to note is a crescent-shaped scar in the grass, and just beyond this is the quarryman's path.

❽ The path is easily recognised by its by stone paving, so turn left here to follow a long, gentle climb. The path is obvious and heads up to a saddle in the hillside. At the top of the climb you arrive at the crossroads passed after the first climb. Go straight over to descend the same path you initially climbed up. The quarry and pub come into view but watch your step as you speed down on good ground. Cross the small bridge and make your way back to the road and pub to finish.

Roos and Staple Tors – SW

Looking back at Great Staple Tor – SW

5 Peter Tavy High Ground

Distance	10.4km (6.5 miles)
Ascent	407m (1,330ft)
Grade	F2
Start / Finish	Peter Tavy Church SX 513 777 (50.5802 -4.1012)

Important note: While this route does not enter the Merrivale Firing Range, if you wish to undertake the dog-leg out to the Langstone menhir (standing stone), you may only enter when the range is not firing as this extra bit encroaches on to the range. Please check the government website prior to running this route if you intend to visit the stone.

Peter Tavy is one of those quiet rural Dartmoor villages that is steeped in character. It has a proper English pub, a village hall, and a stream running through it. Being only three miles outside the market town of Tavistock, it is conveniently close to grocers, banks, schools, and the like.

While the location is ideal for the everyday, mundane stuff of life, its situation, at the base of some of the most outstanding tors to run over is a major selling point for estate agents. Or at least it should be! For the avid trail and fell runner, the training ground is manna from heaven with steep climbs, long runnable descents and as much or as little technical ground as you wish. Classic Dartmoor mires are few and far between making the running less frustrating. However, depending on your disposition, be warned. Starting a run from Peter Tavy generally involves an uphill gradient, so prepare yourself mentally beforehand so as not to 'throw one's teddy out of the pram' when your pace watch cajoles you to get a move on.

5 Peter Tavy High Ground

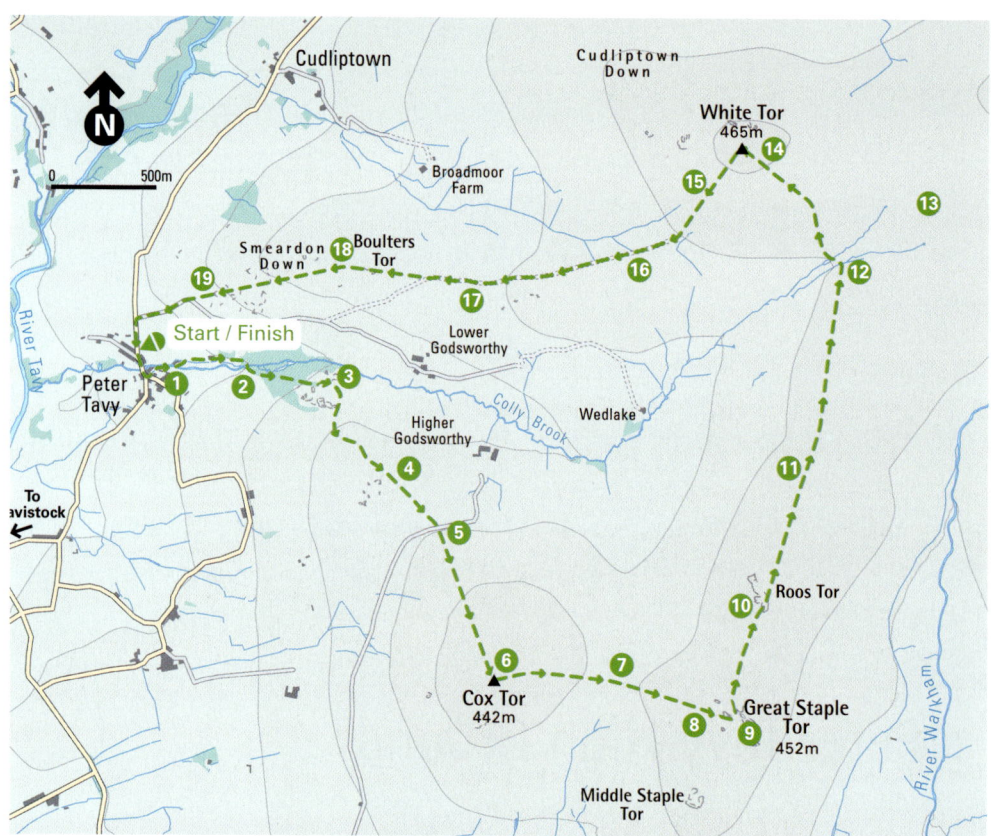

With so much to explore, it seems an injustice to only feature one run from this locality, but the route outlined in this chapter takes in the lion's share of the area's best features without venturing too far.

On the route you will pass an old Victorian bathing pool, still used by the locals today. The pool was recently drained, cleaned and the surrounding trees cutback. This bathing, however, is frowned upon by the Dutchy of Cornwall, upon whose land it resides, due to an unresolved issue of insurance. However, despite the warning sign which says: 'Strictly No Bathing' there is a life ring there, obvious when you undertake this route. Don't be surprised if, when you run past on a warm summer's day, you come across people enjoying the benefits of why it was put there in the first place.

As the route climbs up the tors to the east of the village, each part of this run will show its own unique character, with Logan stones (ones that are balanced precariously and often rock under one's weight), a trig point, boundary stones, a granite 'menhir' (standing stone), a Neolithic enclosure, a young man's grave, and, weather permitting, outstanding 360-degree views.

The Langstone menhir, standing at nearly 3m, on the Old Lych Way (a route along which bodies in coffins were traditionally transported across the parish, to be buried in the Abbey at Tavistock) has seen its fair share of history. The strange cup marks in the stone are not a geological or ancient feature, but one of 20th Century abuse. Prior to the D-Day landings, the stone was used for target practice to sharpen the soldier's accuracy. The stone, not being able to fire back, obviously came off considerably worse in this fire-fight.

Peter Tavy High Ground 5

At this point I should remind you that although most of this run does not enter the Merrivale Firing Range, the dog-leg out to this stone does for a brief time, so check for red flags on the day on the tops of the tors, or consult the website prior to venturing out.

White Tor has some of the best views this side of the moor. To the east and north is the open span of the national park, with Tavy Cleave over to the north-east. Brent Tor with the church perched on top of its volcanic cone over to the north-west. Bodmin Moors rounded peaks over to the west in Cornwall, and the maritime port of Plymouth and the river Tamar over to the south. These incredible vistas cannot have been the reason for the site of the Neolithic settlement beneath your feet, but I am sure it was enjoyed all the same.

Nearing the end, the route passes Stephen's Grave, the final resting place of a young gent, who having been cheated on by his lover, decidided to take his own life. Due to the unholy nature of his death, the local folks, fearful of reprisals from the man's soul, decided he

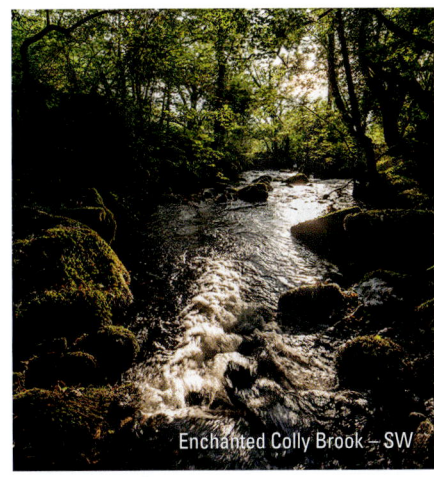

Enchanted Colly Brook – SW

Track heading west – SW

should be buried at the meeting point of three local parish boundaries. Another such grave over on the east side of the moor is of similar nature. Legend is that at night (when else) his ghost, unable to pass into the afterlife, roams this area. Strangely, my pace over this stretch always seems to be quite fast.

Other than on the day of the Summer Fête, the village itself is generally quiet, although on any given Sunday, the Peter Tavy Inn is fully booked for Sunday roasts; testament to its fine reputation for good food and local ales. Despite the fact that there is no car park, parking is generally not a problem. I recommend parking next to the row of houses running adjacent to the church on the roadside, taking care not to block any gate or access. The space before the church is also usable, although expect it to be busy on a Sunday morning. Failing that, ask at the pub, particularly if partaking of its hospitality on completion of the run. The route is generally on good ground with its fair share of sheep tracks and trods to follow. In fine weather, the route is easy to see and adapt as, at any point on this route, if you have had enough, just head back down the valley and back to the village.

Route

From the church, head out of the village past the village hall and follow the stream up on to the moor, via Great Combe Tor and on to Cox Tor and its trig point. Turn left to descend to a pond before climbing again to Great Staple Tor. Left again via Roos Tor to head over to White Tor, via the standing stone if you choose. From White Tor, head for home via Stephen's Grave and Smeardon Down.

5 Peter Tavy High Ground

Detailed directions

START From the towered church, head downhill into the heart of the village and turn left just after crossing the stream to see the village hall and its car park in front of you. A bus shelter complete with notice board sits opposite and a track splits the two so follow this, over a stone step to the right of the stream.

1 Where the path hits a lane turn left over the stream again and follow the lane uphill past a row of quaint terrace houses. The road eventually runs out and is replaced by a stone track which leads to a gate. Go through the gate and at the immediate crossroads take the right fork down to the riverbank where a footbridge comes into view.

2 Cross over the bridge and follow the often muddy and always rocky path as it turns left through the trees and then keep right past the bathing pool, still climbing gently. The trees get left behind as the path rises and the first rocky outcrop comes into view on the right. Take care here as the stones underfoot between the grassy tufts are polished and slippery.

3 As the gradient eases a wall crossing in front comes into view, so swing right following the faint trod keeping the crag to your right. Follow the line of the wall as it funnels you in between another wall and on to a wide wooden gate, with a large wooden latch. On passing through the gate, bear left and hop over the raised earth bank. Follow the trod up, with the wall just off to your left and another crag coming into view on the right. The trod becomes more obvious as it squeezes through another raised earth bank to meet a wider farm track coming right to left. A wooden signpost confirms your position, although it has seen better days.

4 Turn left on a much easier gradient now, and follow this wide, rutted track to a gate in the far-left corner of the field. The intimidating mass of Cox Tor now comes into view ahead, although not its summit, just its flanks exposing frost shattered clitter.

5 Cross the tarmac farm lane and head straight up an obvious grass path as it heads straight up to a crag, through the bracken. The way is less obvious as it steepens, so just find your best line to crest the summit plateau and you will see a large crag dead in front. This is not the summit, however, as this lies a short distance behind the crag on easier ground.

6 Head over the mogul-like tufts of grass, bearing slightly right and still climbing on an easily runnable slope, to reach the summit of Cox Tor, identified by its concrete triangulation point on top.

7 After taking in the view of the tempting ice cream van in the car park, half a mile below to the south, turn ninety degrees left and descend east towards a pond, which can be dried up in the summer, leaving just a brown, baked crust. A path leads to the pond if you head directly to the largest and highest tor of the three rocky outcrops ahead of you. This is Great Staple Tor and is the middle of what appears to be three prominent tors, and your next destination after the pond.

8 The running here is fast, fun, and easy to follow, but soon climbs again as you leave the pond behind you. Again, a trod shows you the way through the clitter initially but becomes less obvious as you near the summit tors. The gradient is easy and runnable, terrain notwithstanding.

9 On reaching the summit tors, pass the first major outcrop to its right, and then turn left between it and

Peter Tavy High Ground 5

Tavy valley, mist clearing at dawn – SW

another outcrop over to the right. This points you straight at Roos Tor, your next location via a trod, and some clitter with a boundary marker in the saddle below.

🔟 Pass through Roos Tor, often with Dartmoor ponies at its summit as it seems a favourite of theirs, and open moorland opens before you. The terrain now offers a wide ridge with White Tor just to the left of north. This is where we need to head to. Two faint trods like a V-shape are in front, the right falling slightly to the right of the ridge, the left similarly on the left. Each path seems marked by a boundary stone; take the left trod. In the distance a wall is visible coming in from the far left, and its far right-hand corner is where to aim for.

⓫ The trod is good and fast with a generally descending nature. To the right, there should be the flat ridge above you. If you get swept down more to the left, fear not as you will just meet the stone wall. If this occurs turn right and follow it to the corner.

⓬ At the wall corner, a stone track suddenly appears so follow this as it crosses a ford and snakes its way gently left and then right, as it climbs uphill at a runnable gradient. Head straight uphill as the path fades and crosses a significant track stretching from left to right.

⓭ At this point, if you wish to look at the Langstone menhir, turn right and follow this track for a few hundred metres, past a small wooden sign that reads *"no access to military vehicles"*. Return the same way to the same point.

Note: Keen runners and accomplished navigators might at this point question why not head right from Roos Tor and then left to take in the menhir on route? In fine, dry weather this might be an option but at all other times I will give you a one-word explanation, bog. On an orienteering event many years ago, the runner in front of me on his way to White Tor from the east, decided to cut across this way, while I went round. Needless to say, I overtook him and watched as he waded, waist deep, through a classic Dartmoor 'quaker' or soft bog.

⓮ Back now to the track, head uphill towards White Tor and scramble over a low Neolithic wall, which contours around the shallow summit of the tor. Head towards the flagpole in the middle, which is not

5 Peter Tavy High Ground

Dawn over Godswrthy – SW

Neolithic, but is one of the range flags used to indicate if the ranges are in use. Red flag means they are firing, no flag means no firing. Rest assured you are not inside the range here, so safe whatever the flag says.

15 For the final stretch, in misty weather and to play safe, retrace your steps to the previous wide track and turn right and follow. Alternatively, if visibility is good from the flagpole on White Tor, face towards Brent Tor church to the west on the horizon and head south-west down the slope. A large boulder is easily spottable, run towards and then left of it. An obvious trod weaves through the clitter and down a slope before picking up a wider, grassy track. A farm is visible now in the valley, and following the track head in the farms direction until you reappear on the wide, stony track which you crossed earlier.

16 Turn right and descend quickly on easy ground, following the track. A small stone on the left marks the place of George Stephen's grave, marked as Stephen's Grave on most maps. The letter 'S' is etched into the base.

17 Stay on the track downhill as the path becomes fenced in between two stone walls, leaving a narrow channel to pass through. The path at the end of the left-hand wall drops left and back towards the start, but indulge me and instead stay high and follow the faint trod which follows the line of the wall on the right towards a rocky outcrop known as Boulters Tor. Follow the high ground and as the wall turns sharply right, keep straight on, climbing gently through ancient hut circles along to another rocky outcrop.

18 Now, as a reward, nearing the finish and having climbed uphill for most of this run, follow the ridge-line over Smeardon Down, keeping to the right of the rocky crags as a faint but obvious grassy path descends steeper with each step. This is what off-road running is all about.

19 If you have kept your feet and enjoyed yourself, feel free to climb back up and repeat. Failing that, do as I do, hit the tarmacked road and turn right to cross a cattle grid. Follow the lane down and back to the church, where you began.

Watchet Hill and Great Links Tor

6 Okehampton to the Moor and Back

Distance	15.2km (9.5 miles)
Ascent	457m (1500ft)
Grade	T2b
Start / Finish	Simmonds Park SX 589 948 (50.7358 -3.9998)

Okehampton sits just outside the northern edge of Dartmoor and as such seems an ideal place to base yourself for running on the moor. Most folk however, drive up to the fringes and park in one of the many small lay-bys and car parks made available. The reason for this? To avoid the monster climb out of the town, and instead leave something in the tank for the tors and tracks within the national park itself.

I'm not a huge fan of driving, so over the years I have developed a run that starts and finishes in Okehampton, with a more gentle climb suitable for most, and which then finishes with a long, fast descent.

Okehampton is a town that has good facilities, including loos, supermarkets, cafés and bars. Simmonds Park is a lovely place to start a run and has a car park in which to leave your vehicle.

The route itself goes along woodland paths and river valley tracks before climbing up on to moorland trods. The return journey drops off steeply to follow tracks and paths back to the park.

The route also summits one of the highest peaks on the moor, so be prepared for the weather conditions, and although trail shoes would be sufficient, I might consider studded fell shoes in the wetter months.

6 Okehampton to the Moor and Back

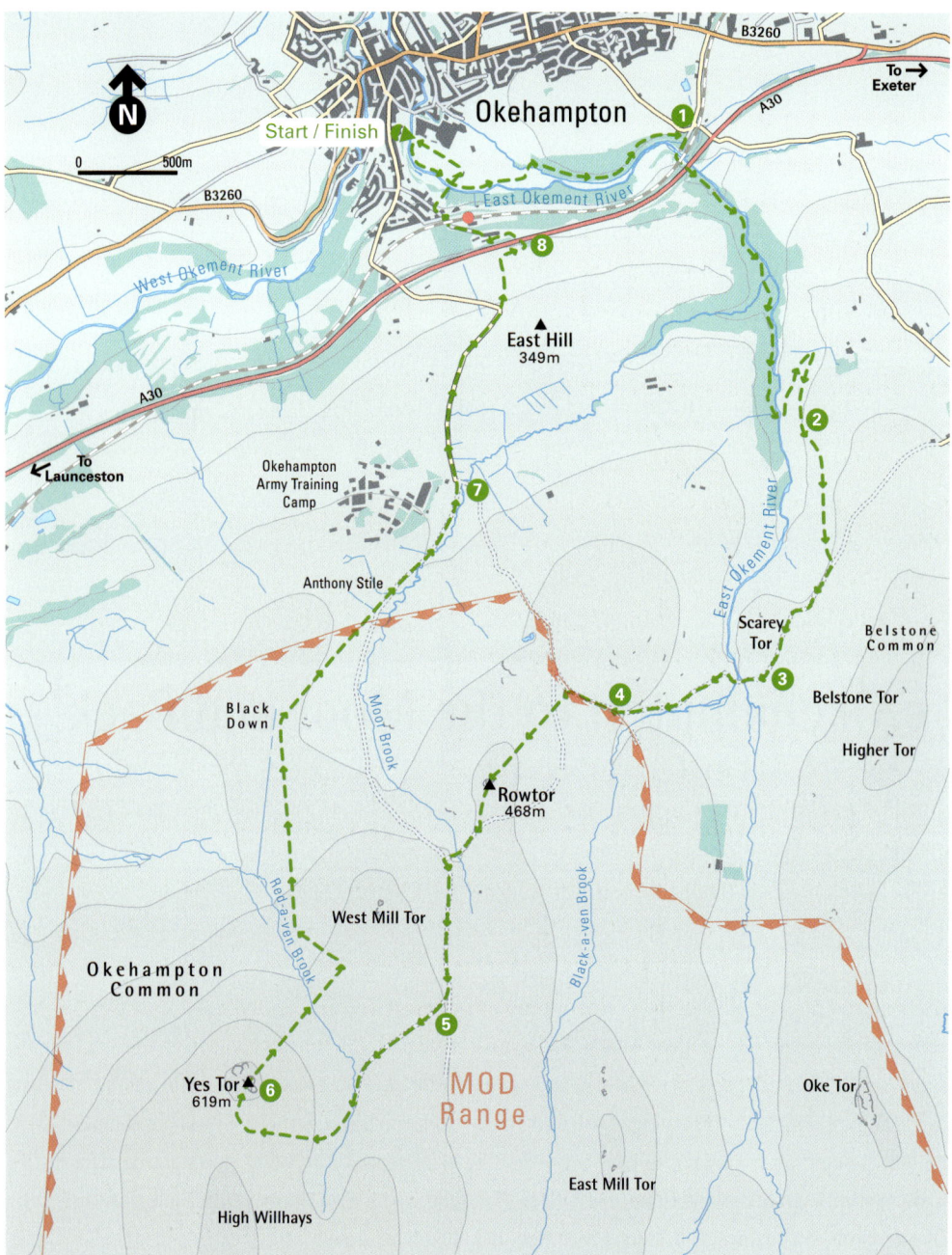

Route

Starting in the car park of Simmonds Park, head east along a path to gain the river and follow upstream on to the moor. Turn right after Scary Tor and cross the river again to climb towards a series of tors. Head across the tors to the summit of Yes Tor, before turning north to follow trods and tracks back towards Okehampton, crossing the rail line and dual carriageway in the process.

Okehampton to the Moor and Back   6

Detailed directions

Railway viaduct

🚶 **START** Starting in the car park within Simmonds Park, stand with your back to the school and play park over to the left. Head straight across the grass to meet the river and turn left to follow the riverbank. Turn sharp left at a fence and follow the path to meet a main path on the other side of a small stream. Turn right and follow the well-maintained path out of the park, accompanied by the constant drone of the main A38 road, high above to the right.

❶ At the end of the path by a gate, turn right to follow the road to the river and cross the bridge. Turn left through the gate and go through the small tunnel under the railway track, then the A38 itself.

❷ The path follows the line of the river upstream on its right bank and climbs gently through woodland. At a path junction or fork, choose the left one and cross a footbridge over a brook. The path returns closer again now to the main river and eventually terminates at a bridge to cross over. Take the bridge, and once over, turn right.

Optional swimming spot

❸ The path is out of the trees now and climbs between the bracken and gorse up to a main track coming in from the left. Turn right here and follow this hard track to the left of a small rocky outcrop called Scarey Tor. This path then meets another junction. Turn right to cross the river again via a bridge or ford, and follow the track uphill, taking the left fork steeply up.

❹ The track meets a road at the top. Turn right here and follow on the flat for a brief time before another track comes in from the left. At this junction, a faint trod leads left across open moorland towards a small hill with a tor (Rowtor) on top. Follow this up and over the summit and descend to a track. Head straight on with another tor directly in-line.

❺ Once across the stream, turn left on to the main track and follow around the tor on the right until you meet a fork. Take the right fork and climb up on to the ridge ahead. Turn right at the top to climb Yes Tor, the second highest tor on the moor.

❻ At the trig point on the top, turn right to descend a faint trod (heading just east of north) down, across a slope full of rock debris. After the stream, turn left and pick up a track heading down a valley to another T-junction. Turn right and follow the track, still going downhill, until it meets a road. Continue straight on down the road, with the small, military, battle camp on the left.

❼ At the bottom of the road, turn left across the cattle grid and then follow the road round the camp to the right. Keep straight on until a small cross on the left, and a tight, left-hand, ninety degree bend comes

6   Okehampton to the Moor and Back

The descent home

into view. At the bend, go straight ahead through a gate, and keeping left of the trees, follow the public footpath down across a field to find a footbridge over the main dual carriageway.

❽ Once across, bear left and follow the footpath until you meet a road where you turn right and go under the railway line. Following the road straight ahead, take the second marked footpath by the edge of some terraced houses on the right and follow the footpath down and back into the park. Turn left at the bottom and then right across the bridge, to access the field opposite the school and where you started from.

Belstone Horseshoe 7

The author guiding on this route. – AF

7 Belstone Horseshoe

Distance	12.8km (8 miles)
Ascent	416m (1567ft)
Grade	F2
Start / Finish	Belstone village SX 621 938 (50.727 -3.9549)

The village of Belstone sits on the northern edge of Dartmoor and is a great location from which to start a run. It boasts a well-stocked pub, called The Tors Inn, which also has rooms for an overnight stay. 'The Shed' situated on the edge of the pub, provides good burgers and a superb alfresco dining experience for tired legs, weather permitting.

If you like proper tea and cake, The Old School Tea Room is situated behind the Chapel. It is open in the afternoons at weekends.

Parking in the village at weekends can cause a lot of teeth-gnashing, but fortunately a car park is provided. On entering the village from the north, it is just on the left opposite the village hall. This also fills up quickly so get there early. If parking here, which I recommend, the start of the run (and the pub), is only 500m away through the village.

The route enters the Okehampton Firing Range, so it is necessary to check firing times before commencing this run.

Once you have established it's all clear to run, you are in for a feast of moorland running. The run itself follows some of the line of the *'International'* Sticklepath Horseshoe Fell Race. The 'International' due to

7 Belstone Horseshoe

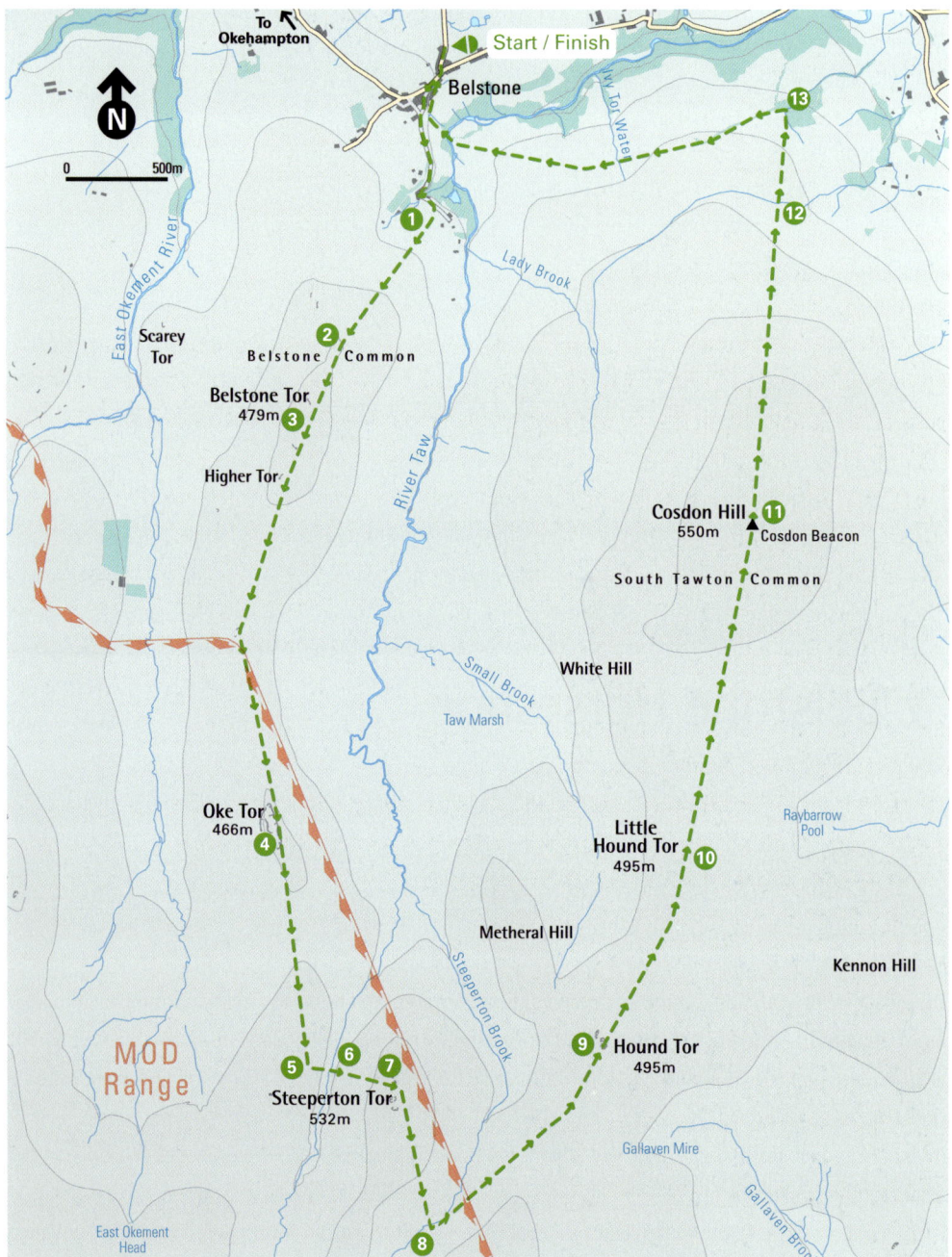

the fact that in recent times, two Italian athletes turned up and ran the race once! Generally, it is a race of fewer than 50 runners, and the runners are all local.

Apart from the fine selection of tors which the route takes in, there are several other interesting features along the way. Notably, Irishman's Wall, Steeperton Gorge, and White Moor Stone Circle.

Irishman's Wall is as straight a stone wall as you could want, and surprising considering its location over the top of Belstone Common. As the name suggests, it is believed that a team of Irishmen built the wall

Belstone Horseshoe 7

as a boundary, having acquired the land on one side. The Belstone locals, upset at the common land being segregated, waited till nightfall and the walls near completion, and then proceeded to set about dismantling it. Having said that, the wall remains in relatively good nick.

Stepperton Gorge

Steeperton Gorge is not as deep as the name suggests and should not be mentioned in the same breath as Cheddar for example. However, for a runner on the moor, this is as deep as you would wish. The joy here lies in the slightly sketchy run down into the gorge, the view down it and the lung-busting climb out. The point at which to turn left and hurtle down is made obvious by one of the many field telephone points on the military ranges.

White Moor Stone Circle, like many on the moor, is well preserved and is one of the most remote out of the fourteen on the moor. It is also the highest at 437m in altitude.

The final hill on the route, Cosdon Hill, while not boasting a tor, has arguably the most ancient archaeological, historic sites on its flanks. It is peppered with cairns, burial mounds, and stone rows, which to my mind, mark out this huge mound as a previously significant, sacred place of old. As a runner, it's a slog whichever way you run up it, and is useful for hill reps. Apart from the aforementioned Sticklepath Horseshoe Fell Race, the local, Okehampton Running Club also have the Cosdon Hill Fell Race every summer, which involves a short sprint up from Belstone and back.

I always find the run up here from Little Hound Tor, the crux of the run, a tough section. It is not steep, not overly long, and the ground is easy, but for some reason I always find this an effort. Bear this in mind but don't be put off. Afterall, this is but a mound of opportunity.

Route

From the pub in the village centre, head south on the road past the green to a gate, before ascending Belstone Tor. Follow the ridge along to Oke Tor, and then on to a track, still heading in a southerly direction. At a range telephone point turn left to descend and cross a stream, then up to Steeperton Tor. Descend to a ford, cross and turn left, then climb steadily to the trig point on top of Cosdon Hill. Carry straight on over, to again descend before turning left at the bottom on tracks back to Belstone.

Detailed directions

START Leaving the pub and village green behind, head out on a road, with the slopes of Belstone Green to your left. The road is walled on the right and soon bends right and then left past quaint houses. Take the right fork uphill to reach a large gate, and the entrance to the moor.

1 A wide, stone track now appears upon passing through the gate and a split in the path is a few steps ahead, dominated by the view up to the heights of Belstone Common and Belstone Tor. Rather than take

7 Belstone Horseshoe

either track right or left, head straight on to climb on open moorland up to the ridge ahead. As this is a popular climb, an obvious trod is soon found, which winds up to the first crag. The going is steep, but easy and a good warm up for your legs.

2 Upon reaching the first summit, continue up to the next crag which is Belstone Tor. The view to the right over the high moorland summits is worth a pause.

3 Follow the ridgeline towards the wall, and cross the low remnants of the wall. Keep on the trod and ridgeline to make Higher Tor. The running is easy, although boulders litter the path so watch your step. The route now descends slightly and at another rocky outcrop, cross into the Okehampton Firing Range. Follow the grassy trod slightly uphill now towards Oke Tor. If you stay on the broad ridge, you cannot really go wrong.

4 Pass Oke Tor on its left flank and take note of the old and new range huts sheltering on the northernmost tip of the Tor. From here, the trod veers right slightly and gently downhill. There is another path that turns sharp right, but ignore this. Instead keep heading south as the track becomes more obvious and wider.

5 This stone track, the remains of the old military road, climbs gently and another track joins it from the right. At this junction, a field telephone point marks the place where the run turns sharp left.

6 The path is steep and finishes at a stream in the gorge below, so unless you want to fall in face first, descend under control. Crossing the stream is relatively straight forward, and if you have a keen eye, can find some good crossing boulders without the need to get wet.

7 Instantly, upon crossing, you will be faced with a steep climb, too steep to run, but a good trod leads the way. The effort is short-lived however, and the slope relents in steepness to a more runnable gradient. Head for the range hut which sits on top of Steeperton Tor.

8 At the summit, turn half right and follow a trod downhill, roughly in-line with the range poles, to a ford and stream crossing. Once across, the path turns left and climbs steadily up. At this point, there is the option of staying on this trod, which contours around to the left of the next tor, but I recommend keeping right and climbing up to Hound Tor.

9 From the summit, the way is obvious, so bear left along good paths and the broad ridge. Just off to the right of the route, a slight deviation takes in the well-preserved White Moor Stone Circle.

10 The path takes in Little Hound Tor, and then briefly descends before the long climb up to Cosdon Hill. It is a slog, I won't lie, but frustratingly runnable. At the top is Cosdon Beacon and a trig point, surrounded by stone cairns and shelters.

11 Once recovered, head straight on, via easy trods to another cairn and then reap your reward with a long descent. Keep in mind the need to bear left and not be swept down the steeper slope over to the right, and the village of South Zeal below.

12 At a wall corner, reached in no time at all after the downhill fun, follow the wall on its left, still heading downhill. The boundary wall turns left across your path, follow its line before picking up a good track.

13 Heading westerly now, follow this track through a couple of low streams before it starts to descend and head to the right. The green of Belstone should now be in sight briefly, before the path dives down following the wall line to a wide river ford. Either splash through, or turn left to use the dry footbridge,

14 On reaching the other side, follow the path left and then sharply right as it climbs back to the green and the welcome sight of the pub.

South West

The South West of Dartmoor is a transitional landscape, influenced in part by its closer proximity to the coast and to an even greater extent by the higher population density, including the 'Ocean City' of Plymouth, located just out of the national park's boundary. The upland moorlands start to give way to more industry and farmland, old and new, and the light greens and browns which characterise the North West, make way for deeper greens as streams and rivers all haste south to the sea. Deep, wooded valleys stretch either side of these rivers and offer more opportunities for shelter in poor weather.

Black Tor (Route 10) – SW

Hart Tor (Route 9) – SW

The Dewer to Pay 8

Plantation near the Plym valley

8 The Dewer to Pay

Distance	5.6km (3.5 miles)
Ascent	181m (594ft)
Grade	T1b
Start / Finish	Cadover Bridge SX 554 644 (50.4623 -4.0385)

This is one of the shorter routes in this guidebook, but be advised, it is not a route for personal bests and quick times. In places, this is a technical route with rocks, tree roots and a broken pipeline scattered over what is often a narrow path. On top of that, the grand views and scenery are enough to distract the unwary. On first attempt, as you will want to return to this route on more than one occasion, I would advise you to ease off the gas and instead enjoy the ride. In any case, the steep climb at the halfway point will soon give the cardio junkies their shot in the arm. Or should that be quads?

Hopefully I have whetted your appetite, rather than put you off. This run is ideal as an early morning jaunt, with a deserted car park, the moist breath of the trees rising off the canopy below the Dewerstone Rock, and the feeling of pious satisfaction having just powered your way to the top of the climb before the ice cream and picnic hungry masses have descended to dip their toes in the River Plym.

The area is steeped in legend and history, as much as any other part of the national park. The Dewerstone Rock being the legendary residing place of the Dewer, or Devil, himself. At night he is thought to ride atop his black horse willing on his ghoulish dewerhounds, rounding up sinners from across the moor, back to his rock, before driving them off the summit and sending them crashing down to the river valley below.

8 The Dewer to Pay

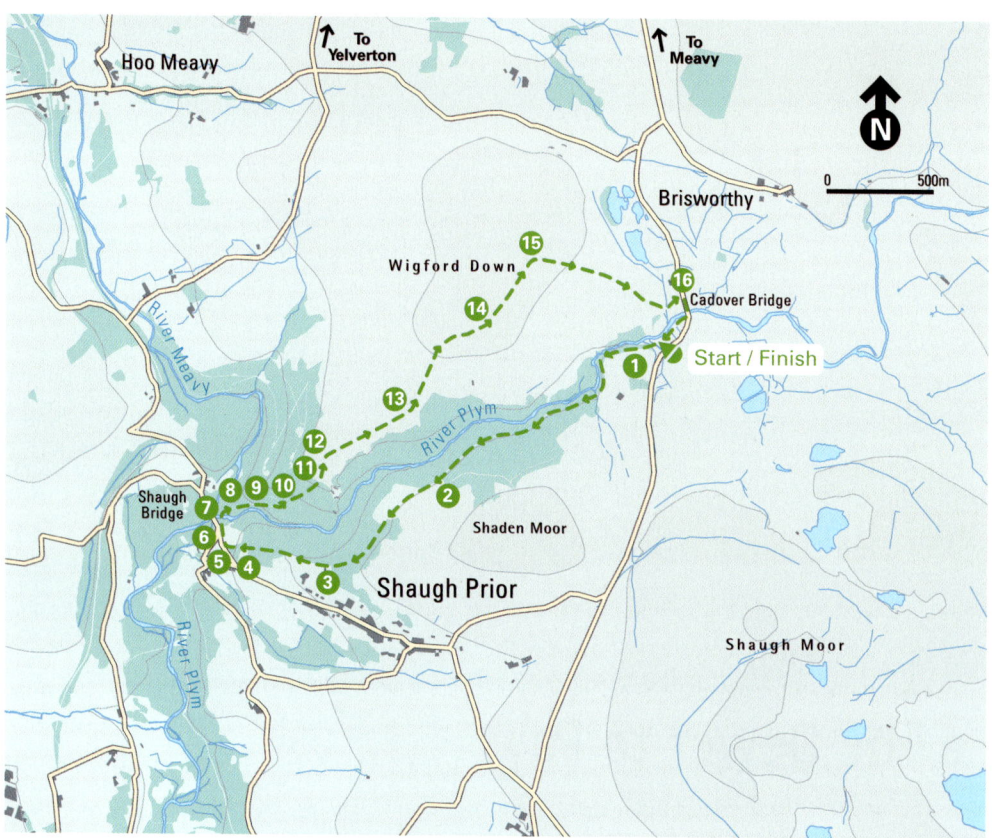

More tangible history is also plentiful on this run, with many industrial remains scattered over the area. The broken pipe, which is laid down on the first half of the run, was used to transport the china clay slurry from the nearby quarries at the start of the run, which are still present in some form today. The china clay drying sheds, built from 1870 and last used in 1952 at the halfway point are further evidence of such industry in the past. The carts used to back into the bays, collect the dry, china clay and transport it to the nearby railway. (www.heritagegateway.org.uk – HER number MDV2218)

The Dewerstone Iron Mine has also left behind ruins such as the 19th century, old smithy, just at the start of the steep climb.

Cadover Cross, passed near the end of this run, stands over 2m high and served as a waymarker for monks travelling between priories. It dates from the 1200s, but has been restored and stood up many times since. However, more recent history of this area is much closer to my heart and its relative proximity to the military base just up the road at Bickleigh. When serving personnel were still paid weekly in cash by the unit paymaster, the earnings were only handed over once the soldiers serving at the barracks had run from the gate to the top of the Dewerstone on pay day. Royal Marine folklore maintains that this weekly ritual was hotly contested and the last man to the top was forced to forego his wages, the sum instead donated to the mess's beer fund. The facts and truth of this story are hard to source and, like the Dewer himself, potentially only myth. When I asked a fellow veteran, well versed in the Royal Marines tales of old, for verification, he would only answer: *"Why let the truth get in the way of a good story?"*

The Dewer to Pay

River Plym - SW

However, as was tradition, it was from this camp in late February 2011 that yours truly ran with the rest of 42 Commando Royal Marines, to the summit of the Dewerstone, to take part in a final, outdoor service conducted by the unit Chaplain, before deploying on operations to Afghanistan. Seven brothers in arms would not return to ever see these views, and many more would be unable to run up its slopes again with such ease. The padre handed out small combat crosses, to attach to our identity tags, at the end of the service to those who believed and many to those who did not, but hedged their bets anyway. I have mine to this day. I have yet to, and probably never will, forget that day and those who I knew personally who would not return. Every time I huff and puff my way to the summit through the trees, my shortness of breath reminds me that I am fortunate to still feel it.

The car park at the start is of good size and free, but can be overrun in the summer with visitors from Plymouth, so if planning this route, start early to get a spot. There is an ice cream van here most of the year, but do not rely on it as sustenance. They only take cash as there is little, or no, phone signal.

The River Plym is shallow most of the year but deep enough to swim in under the bridge for those who want to cool off after the run.

The nearby village of Shaugh Prior, a mile or so to the south of the car park has a good pub called the White Thorn and serves good pub grub. If you eat in the garden, you might have to share with the resident goats who roam free and do, on occasion, climb on the tables.

There are no loos at the start or on route.

Route

From the substantial Cadover car park, head south-west along the southern bank of the River Plym on narrow, technical paths to Shaugh Bridge. Cross over the river on the bridge provided and follow the path up stream, climbing steeply to the Dewerstone rocks. Return via Oxen Tor to Cadover Cross, over open moorland before crossing back over the river and back to the start.

8 The Dewer to Pay

Detailed directions

START Leaving the car park with the river on your right, make for a kissing gate in amongst a gathering of shrubs and bushes in the south corner.

1 The path leads into North Wood, predominantly oak trees, and follows an old pipe, much of which has been destroyed but is present enough to be obvious and so offers a more technical run.

2 After approximately a mile, you will leave the wood via a gate but continue on the path which opens up to offer outstanding views of the Dewerstone Rock over to the right, a favourite spot for climbers. Over to the left, views of Staddon Heights to the south of Plymouth can be seen, way off in the distance.

3 On reaching a ruin on the right, take the right fork in the path down to a gate, marking the edge of Shaugh Prior village. Leaving the gate closed, instead follow the fingerpost sign, and stay to the right of the fence, avoiding the road and houses to the left. This path is narrow and steep, with many tree roots, the nemesis of any trail runner particularly in the wet, so take care.

4 Go through another gate and keep to the left of the ruins of the old china clay drying sheds, descending all the time.

5 Follow the path towards the road and then swing right at its very edge to come to the top of a very steep flight of narrow stoned steps. Twinkletoes are a must here!

6 The steps lead to a car park at the base of the ruins, an alternative place to park if you wish to start the route from here.

7 Turn right and go through the car park to the far end, past the notice board and cross the River Plym using the wooden bridge.

8 Bearing right, follow the wide, steep stone path uphill and past the old iron smithy. The long, steep climb now begins.

9 Ignoring all the minor paths, particularly the first on the right which leads to the base of the climbing area, keep to the main path which zigzags, always uphill.

10 The stone path now disappears and is replaced by a steep, narrow path which goes slightly left and directly uphill. Well done if you are still running at this stage.

11 The path soon emerges from the treeline and crosses a stone wall, to reveal the summit of the Dewerstone Rock, a few bounds ahead.

12 Enjoy the 360-degree views from the summit, including the military camp over to the south west.

13 Turning right from the original ascent, you will see a path stretching out to Oxen Tor, also known as Cadworthy Tor, to the north-east along a wide ridge-line. Head towards the tor on a grassy path and meet a stone wall.

14 Turn left and follow the boundary wall, then stay with it as it swings right to run parallel with the contours and hillside.

15 As the wall turns right and descends, Cadover Cross comes into view, and passing this follow the faint path to the right of a house and meet the road.

16 Turn right to cross the bridge and turn immediately right again upon crossing to pick up the green banks of the River Plym, maybe with enough time for a dip before returning to the car park.

Ditsworthy Warren House   9

Ditsworthy Warren House – SW

9 Ditsworthy Warren House

Distance	6.4km (4 miles)
Ascent	150m (490ft)
Grade	T1
Start / Finish	Gutter Tor Refuge car park SX 578 673 (50.4882 -4.0048)

This run brings back the odd shudder of bad memories from recruit training in these parts. The building known as Gutter Tor Refuge next to the car park was used as a base for a week or more's training in the surrounding area, mainly for navigation skills. The mire just in front was a popular re-enforcement tool for the memory if you had either performed badly or just needed the skills taught the day before reiterated. Trust me, the mire is grim and, although not a standard teaching aid available in most educational establishments, it seemed to work wonders for the memory and sharpening of skills.

Perhaps it was with this in mind that Steven Spielberg decided to use the area as a setting for his film: Warhorse. Ditsworthy Warren House and the area in front by the river was used to stage the battlefields of the First World War. If you have watched the film, you may recognise the building. This run goes past the house itself, now boarded up and used by the MOD for training purposes.

One key feature of note on the route is the tallest standing stone, or menhir, on Dartmoor, at 14 feet in height, in a place called Drizzle Combe. This is just on the hill up from the house, and is a key point to navigate from when climbing the tor ahead.

9 Ditsworthy Warren House

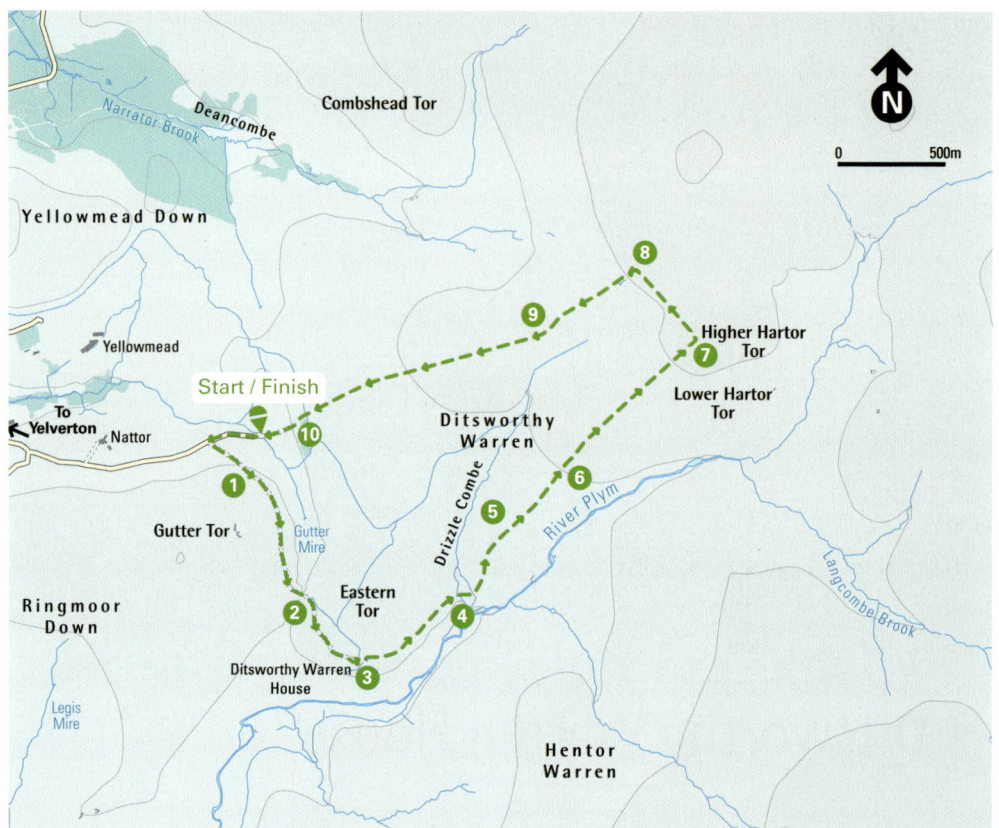

The run itself is a great, uncomplicated moorland run and gives the beginner a taste of the moorland itself without straying far from the safety of the car park.

Route

From the small car park head south on a good, hard vehicle track to Ditsworthy Warren House, keeping the mire on your left. Take the track left of the house itself as it now turns north-east and follow uphill to the summit of Higher Hartor Tor. Turn left to head to an obvious track. Turn left again and follow the track downhill back to the car park to complete the full square.

Detailed directions

START Turning your back on the trees surrounding the refuge, follow the road to the cattle grid and gate, and without crossing, turn left here on to a broad track. Follow this under the flanks of Gutter Tor, to your right on the other side of the fence, and make for the metal gate ahead.

① Pass to the right of the gate, through a small gap and continue on the wide track in a southerly direction. Gutter Mire, over to the left, makes you appreciate the good ground and the track swings left to cross the mires outlet stream, still on the good ground.

Ditsworthy Warren House   9

Higher Hartor Tor – SW

❷ After a slight incline, the track bears right and south again, and starts to descend, with views over to Hen Tor ahead on the hillside, and the River Plym in the valley. A roof starts to appear over to the left and the track creeps left to reveal the uninhabited Ditsworthy Warren House. Head this way and explore at your leisure.

❸ The track now continues left of the house, and leaving it behind follow the good, but now less well-maintained track as it passes a sign saying, "No Troops beyond this point". Unless you are a 'Troop' of Royal Marine recruits in uniform or similar, carry on, as the path descends to a ford.

❹ There are stones to aid the crossing this braided-type ford of the fantastically named Drizzle Combe, and in the summer, this is little more than a trickle. However, be prepared for a wet foot or two most times of the year.

A distant Lower Hartor Tor – SW

❺ The way ahead is now on grass tracks which lead to the obvious landmark of a tall standing stone, marking the start of a stone row. Another, taller standing stone marks the other end and points your direction uphill on a selection of good grass tracks, all leading to the same place, the summit, and Higher Hartor Tor.

Higher Hartor Tor – SW

❻ The path leads through ancient round settlements which are obvious, and complete with entrances. The gradient is not steep and is runnable for the fit but is longer than you think as the summit tor is hidden. Cross the low, outer boundary wall of the settlement and continue up as the tor comes into view.

9 Ditsworthy Warren House

Gutter Tor – SW

7 Higher Hartor Tor has a lowly demeaner, but the views back down the hill towards Plymouth are worth a look. Facing uphill again, pass through the tor and turn left at a large boulder to see a clear grass path, leading to another boulder in a small dip or re-entrant. Cross through what is no more than a ditch, and make for the pair of stone pillars marking an old doorway up ahead. Pass through the remains of a more modern settlement than previously encountered on this run, and reach a wide track going from right to left. The remains are of Eylesbarrow Tin Mine.

8 This is known as Jobbers Lane; turn left here on a good track, popular with mountain bikers, to descend gently. Ground and bikers allowing, peer over to the right to see a plethora of tors to the north, including Combshead Tor in the foreground, and Leather Tor, Sharpitor and Leedon Tor further left and in the distance. See of you can spot the small triangle of Brent Tor and its church on top in the far distance, the huge, buffalo-shape mound further left and closest is Sheeps Tor, which dominates the view as you continue to descend on the track.

9 Navigation here is easy, so quicken the pace in a stiff wind, as this is quite an exposed area, or ease off and take in the views. The gentle rise in the track as it passes a boundary stone on your right is just a mere hiccup, and soon the track steepens again as the coniferous trees which come in to view signal the point at which you started this run.

10 Pass the refuge or hut to its right, still on the same, good track, and finally cross the bridge, or ford to return to the beginning.

Crazy Well Loop 10

10 Crazy Well Loop

Distance	8km (5 miles)
Ascent	212m (696ft)
Grade	T1b
Start / Finish	Norsworthy Bridge car park SX 568 693 (50.5061 -4.0198)

Burrator Reservoir is a popular spot for tourists, and the lane which goes around it has become a staple for London Marathon training, being flat and 4 miles per loop. Granted, the surrounding vista is amazing, being surrounded by tors and a large expanse of water but running on-road brings me out in a rash, and doing laps is just heinous.

This route leaves the roadies to themselves and goes off, into the wild. The route is uncomplicated by Dartmoor standards, and can be followed in most weathers. Two tors are taken in on this run, a couple of stone rows and a large pool, ideal for wild swimming.

Crazy Well Pool is a remnant of the mining industry on the moor, and is full all year-round. It has its own legends, as does most of Dartmoor, one being related to its depth. It was once said that it would take the length of each bell ringing rope from the church at Sheepstor, tied together, to reach the bottom. In the winter, it is frequently frozen over so choose your swimming days carefully.

10 Crazy Well Loop

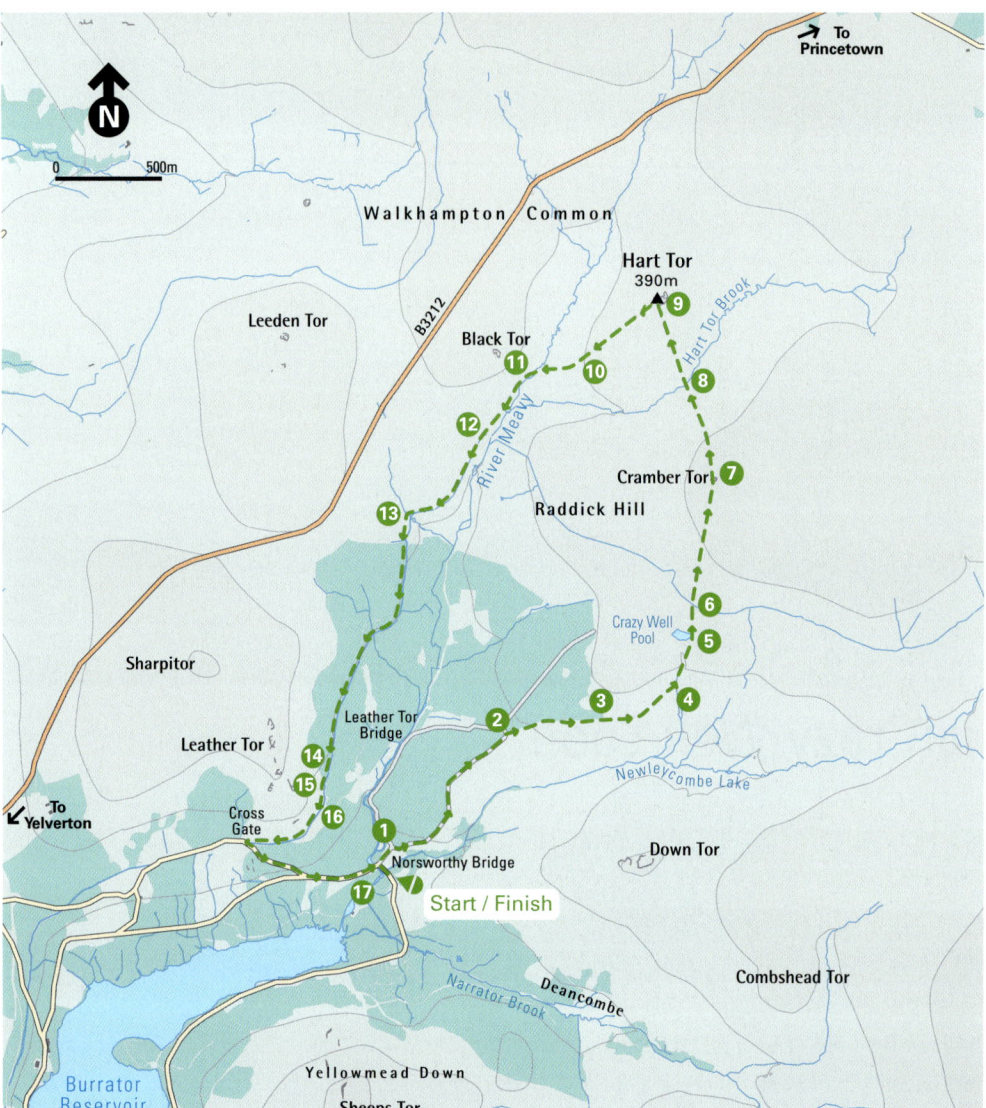

Route

From Norsworthy car park, turn right across the bridge and right again to follow the broad track. At the end of the plantation turn left uphill to Crazy Well Pool then past Cramber Tor, and on to the summit of Hart Tor beyond. Head SW and pass under Black Tor before turning left to follow a leat and paths back to the start.

Detailed directions

START On leaving the car park turn right along the road over a stream until the road turns sharp left over another bridge. At this point, at a makeshift layby on the right, turn right and head up a wide stone track with a slight gradient.

Crazy Well Loop   10

Black Tor – SW

River Meavy, Leather Tor – SW

The Devonport Leat – SW

❶ A path is signposted on the left, into the woods over a stile, but instead stay right and head uphill along the outside edge of the plantation. Beware, as this route is a popular downhill ride for the mountain bikers, it is much easier for you to move out of their way than it is for them to take evasive action.

❷ The wide track is easy going as it hugs the edge of the forest on your left. A clearing appears after less than a mile with a junction offering a track left into the trees, but once again stay right as the gradient eases and starts to run with the contours.

❸ Leaving the plantation now at its edge on your left, head on the same good track, with wide views ahead and on your right of open moorland and granite tors. As the track climbs and sways slightly left look ahead to a large granite cross, a rough guide of where you are heading next.

❹ At a small stream crossing, from the obvious mine, with earth workings to your left on the slope above, turn left off the wide track and follow either left or right of this wide, man-made gulley, now on smaller but still obvious paths.

❺ The cross is now over to your right, as you climb up the path to reach a large pool set in the hillside. This south side of the pool is the best point at which to enter for a swim if tempted.

Crazy Well Loop

6 Follow to the right of the pool now, still gently climbing to gain a path which leads directly up to a leat, where an obvious footbridge made from three blocks of stone allows you to cross. A clear path through the 'tussock grass' leads uphill, away from the bridge, and after a short while bears left towards the obvious blocks of Cramber Tor. Don't be fooled by its position, as even though this is not the top of this particular hill, that being marked by a trig point over to the right, this is the correct spot, and right tor. **Note:** Not all tors are on the summits of peaks on Dartmoor.

7 Carrying on in a straight line over the tor, aiming for the large mast, the path continues finally downhill at speed over soft ground, focusing now on the next tor in the foreground.

8 Cross the brook, with a leap or paddle, in the small valley and, as the next tor is now obscured by the slope ahead, instead aim for the obvious large round boulder. A clear trod takes you past the boulder and up the slope, and on to Hart Tor.

9 From the tor, head south-west and follow the obvious grass path over some gentle clitter and down towards the river as it flows in from the right.

10 The path comes to a stone row after only a few hundred metres. Follow this double stone row downhill and right to meet the river.

11 For easy running, it is best to cross the low ford in the river here, and immediately turn left to descend under Black Tor on your right, following the river downstream until it encounters the Devonport Leat. If you prefer a technical run, then don't cross here, but instead turn left and follow the river on this bank, picking your way over granite debris, left by the workings here. The reward is an old ruin of a blowing house and a close-up view of a waterfall. You will still need to cross the river so choose your spot. It is generally crossable in all but the worst of weathers.

12 Leaving the river, to flow beneath the aqueduct, Monty Python's, Life of Brian fans, may now oblige: *"What have the Roman's ever given us?"*, follow instead the leat downstream, my choice being to do so on the right-hand side as you head south. Both sides give easy running, but I prefer the right. It's your call.

13 The gentle downhill gradient encourages a good pace as does the easy ground and route-finding, as you use the leat's superb engineering to contour the hillside. Upon meeting the fence ahead, cross to the left-hand side to pass through a gate and onwards on a good path as the route re-enters the plantation.

14 Still following the leat downhill, make sure to stay on this path, ignoring all others on the left and right until you reach another gate. As the leat quickens its pace, and the slope steepens, you will notice the increased noise of the leat to your right as it gathers momentum.

15 Continue through the gate and follow the leat until it meets a road. Turn left, downhill, on the road and left again at the bottom to follow the road back to the start.

11 The Neolithic Route

Great Mis Tor – SW

11 The Neolithic Route

Distance	9km (5.6 miles)
Ascent	336m (1,102ft)
Grade	F2
Start / Finish	Four Winds car park SX 560 749 (50.5560 -4.0335)

Some routes on Dartmoor are not to be attempted in the infamous mist, but this one is relatively easy to follow in all weathers. It climbs up to a tor over 500m above sea level, and does involve a river crossing, although this is shallow in most conditions at the crossing point.

The run has numerous points of interest along the way for a leisurely paced loop, including the impressive Mesolithic, or early Bronze Age, parallel stone rows. Their usage is still not fully understood, and like many on Dartmoor, are in really good condition. They still play a significant part of the Druidry religion, and it's not uncommon on a summer solstice to see a few making the pilgrimage here.

The start of the run is the former site of Foggintor School, allegedly housing sixty pupils at one time in the late 1800s, rising to over ninety by the beginning of the 1900s. It closed soon after inspectors, deciding that conditions of overcrowding, poor state of desks and the rather alarming fact that the roof blew off in a storm, were enough to move the pupils to a new school a short distance away. The coniferous tree situated in the wall at the bottom is the remnant of the school Christmas tree.

Merrivale Quarry, the former employer of many from the local settlements in the area is now closed, but the buildings still remain.

11 The Neolithic Route

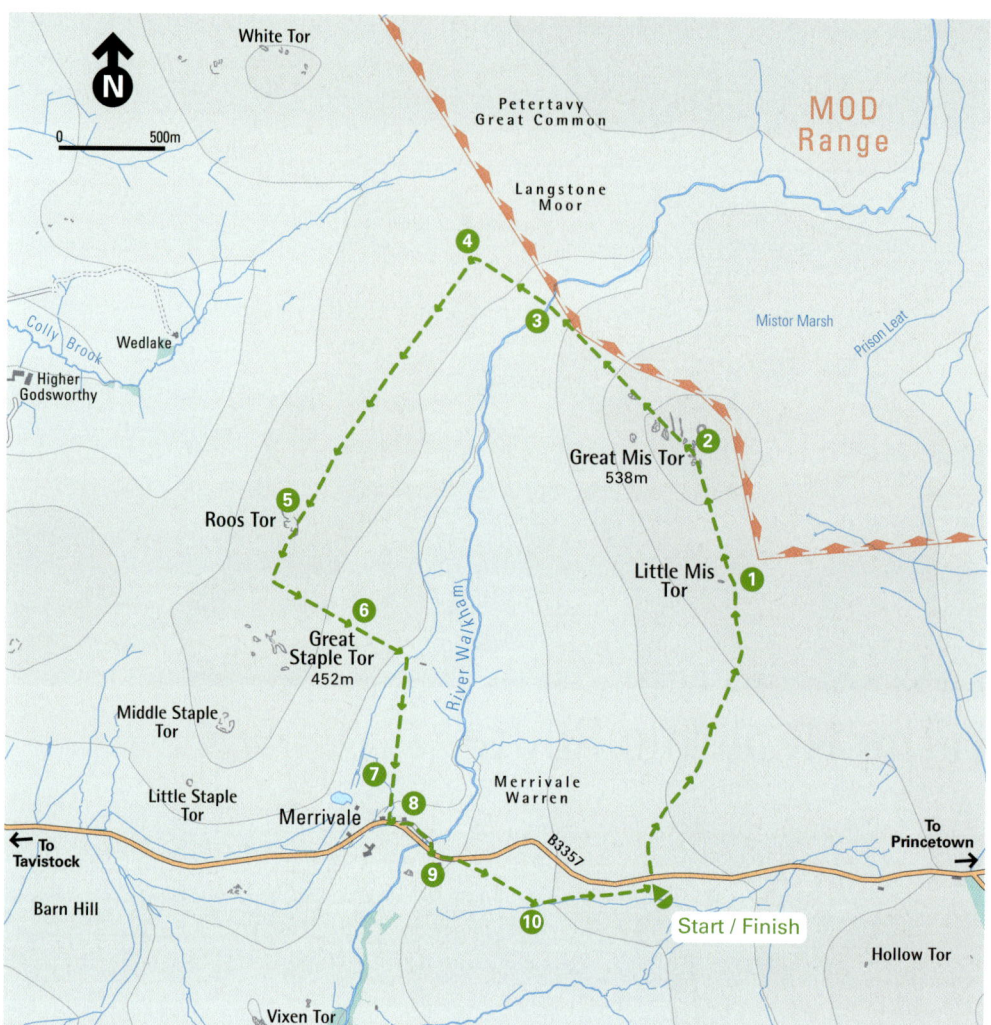

Route

Head north across the road to the summit of a large tor (Great Mis Tor), before turning left to descend to a river. Cross, and once up the steep bank, turn left to follow an uphill track heading up to Roos Tor. Pass through the tor and descend to the saddle and boundary stone. Turn left down a steep track to pick up a farm track heading right and down to the road. Turn left to cross the bridge and then regain the moorland, by heading right to gain the stone rows and then uphill back to the start.

Detailed directions

START Leave the car park to the rear and cross the main Tavistock to Princetown road. Turn right slightly for a few yards to gain a wide, stone vehicle track which ascends north towards the tor on the skyline.

The Neolithic Route — 11

Snowy ponies – SW

① The gradient is slight but consistent, the ground is good and the route following easy. After roughly a mile, the good path peters out at Little Mis Tor, not to be confused with any of the children's books. From here, military vehicle access is prohibited and the path reflects this underfoot.

② However, as with most climbs to any popular tor on Dartmoor, there is still an obvious path to follow, which leads just to the right of the summit of Great Mis Tor. The summit is easily gained with a scramble and there are lots of other rock formations to explore.

③ Exploration complete, head in the same direction as your final approach to the tor, due north, and dropping slightly left, gain a thin trod that follows the line of red and white range poles. Turn left and follow this downhill, over the sometimes rough clitter, all the way to the River Walkham. Take care to stay to the left, so as not to enter the range.

④ Cross the river at an obvious low ford just to the left of the poles, and immediately climb the other side of the valley for less than 500m. On reaching the flat ground, turn left on to a wide grass trod which heads south-west and gently rises to a tor in the distance.

⑤ After what seems like a hard pull, pass through the middle of Roos Tor to descend steeply to the saddle

Merrivale Stones – SW

Merrivale – SW

11 The Neolithic Route

Merrivale Stones at sunset – SW

below, via one of the many well-defined trods. The paths all converge on a boundary stone, and turn immediately left and downhill.

6 The welcome descent follows a good line on a well-worn trod and leads to a stone wall corner. Follow the wall down to reach a more defined vehicle track and turn right, away from the farm.

7 Follow this on good, hard ground and as you approach Merrivale Quarry veer left, to follow the wall on your left down a grass trod which crosses a stream and skirts left of the quarry deposits. A grass path leads to a house on the main road where you turn left.

8 The Dartmoor Inn is now on your left, a great spot, on completion of this run, for a beer or some food. Meanwhile follow the lane in front of the pub, avoiding the main road, and cross the old bridge over the river. Climb the stile at the end, being careful as this leads back on to the main road.

9 Cross the road here and turn left. Keeping in to the right-hand side, follow the road uphill for 100 metres or so to a wall corner. A path then leads up the steep bank to the right, at a diagonal, pointing directly in the direction of the radio mast on top of North Hessary Tor.

10 This faint path, through the 'tussock grass', takes you directly to the Merrivale Stones, situated either side of the small stream. Turn left to climb steadily, along the row of stones following an obvious grass path, which takes you directly back to the trees surrounding the car park and finish.

Gutter Tor – SW

12 Burrator Horseshoe

Distance	9.6km (6 miles)
Ascent	306m (1,005ft)
Grade	F2
Start / Finish	Meavy village green SX 540 671 (50.4862 -4.0582)

This route follows the line of Dartmoor's classic race of the same name. The race, normally on the day of the Meavy Oak fair, a traditional country village fête set on the small green, has been on the race calendar for 25 years. It was set up to raise funds for the fair. Initially the race was exceptionally low key and there have been numerous stories of a laissez faire attitude to the entries and results. Many of today's races have digital chip timing and the like, but this race remains 'old school', with a good, old stopwatch, in keeping with the fair's very English charm.

The fastest time, held by Mark Croasdale RM to this day, is often playfully disputed, as the timing was taken from the race organiser's analogue watch. Some have gone even further to say that the timing was taken from the village church clock, the race organiser, timekeeper, race starter, prize giver (being the one and same chap) was allegedly still in the Royal Oak pub across the green, finishing his pint(s). Do not worry, the gent in question is a top bloke and one of my running buddies so he will not mind the stick!

One year, while checking the course, a cow was found to be in labour directly in the way of the best racing line off Gutter Tor. The cow understandably would not be moved, and became quite aggressive when

12 Burrator Horseshoe

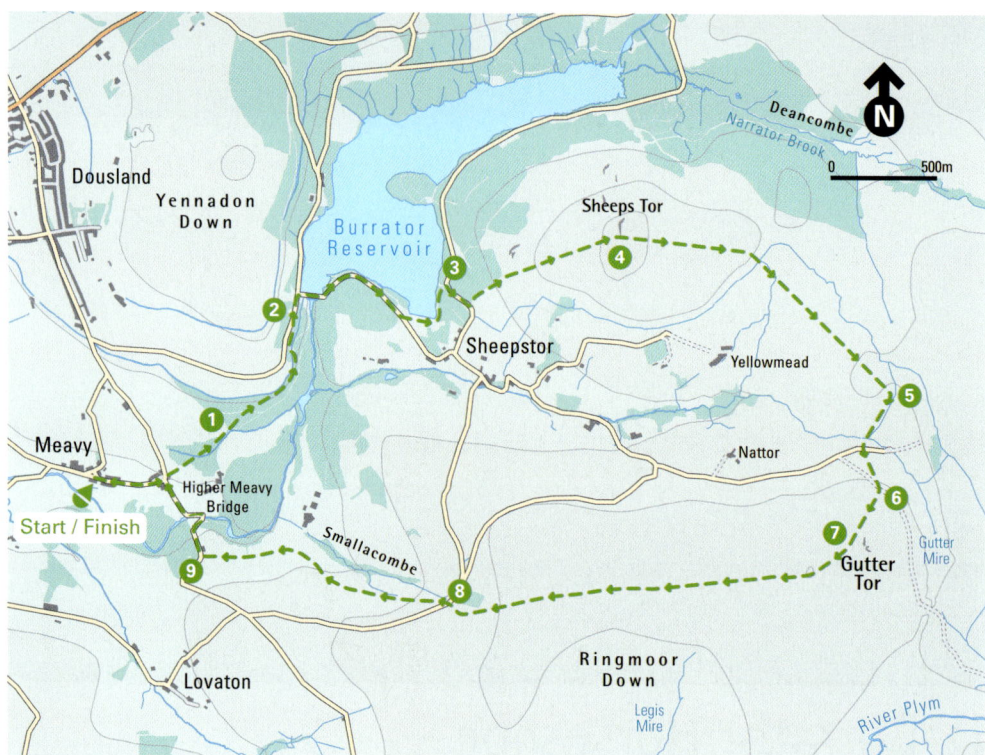

approached, and all runners were warned to take a wide path around the expectant mother. Despite the extra detour, times were found to be significantly quicker over that section!

The original race organiser has now passed the baton on, and the event is now organised by the two local running clubs and the local running store. The run starts from the village of Meavy, which boasts a primary school, church, village hall and the ever-essential Royal Oak Inn. Parking is sparse, with no car park, other than the village hall, but this is generally out of bounds. However, space opposite the pub, by the roadside is usually vacant, as is opposite the primary school at the northern end of the village. The Royal Oak is a great supporter of the race and Oak Fair, and will happily explain the race if you feel some more knowledge is required.

Key features on the route are the Burrator Reservoir Dam and two significant tors: Sheeps Tor and Gutter Tor. However, despite these two climbs, the route itself is very runnable, and fast. The fastest time for a lap of the route currently stands at 37minutes and 47 seconds.

The route is easy to follow and a great place to run without venturing too far into the wilderness. The Royal Oak is very welcoming at any time of year, whether it be a cold shandy on the green outside in the summer, or a pint of bitter by the fire in the winter supplemented by a bowl of chips.

Route

From the village green, head out east on roads, across fields and on tracks making for the reservoir. Turn right and cross the dam, following a road and paths before climbing to the top of Sheeps Tor. Descend the

Burrator Horseshoe 12

Burrator Reservoir from Sheeps Tor

other side to a stream and turn right to climb Gutter Tor. Onwards, past the trig point and follow the moorland path north to the lane leading back to the start.

Detailed directions

START Start on the village green facing the pub, and turn right to run up the lane, past the village hall on the right. Just past the primary school, the road ends at a T-junction. Straight ahead, to the left of a building is a gate, and the route follows the footpath through this. Carry on across the field, to the right of a line of trees, to another two gates in quick succession.

❶ After the second gate, take the left fork uphill along an obvious path between trees. The path climbs up to reach a dry leat. Follow to the right along the edge of the leat to meet a path junction. Head up left again, uphill to a gate which comes out on to a road by some loos. Please note these are pay per use.

❷ Head straight on the road, to the left edge of the dam and turn right to cross the dam, still on the road. This bends hard left, then right, but after a short while, a stile on the left gives access to a waterside path. Cross the stile and turn right to follow through trees to another, smaller dam, which the path crosses. Follow the path left around the reservoir to a gate.

Spot for a breather on the steep climb

Leaving Sheeps Tor

Stone cross on the path

Burrator Horseshoe

3 Go through the gate, and turn right along the road, until the road turns sharply right. A signposted path on the left shows a track heading uphill to another gate. Once through, now on to open moorland, head straight up the western flanks of Sheeps Tor. The first bit is steep, but then eases, before a final, steep scramble to the summit. There are obvious lines up the slope but pick your own.

4 At the top, head straight over, down a grassy path towards the corner of a wall. Do not be tempted to stray left to the planation, or too far right to a road. The going is fast, and the ground makes for a superb descent on lush grass. At the wall corner, follow around to the left and down on a faint path to a stream which you can cross easily. The path is obvious and follows the line of the wall on the right, climbing gently.

5 At the end of the wall, the path becomes more obvious, and swings right following the line of the wall. It is tempting to head straight over to the building ahead, known as the Scout Hut, but the ground here is extremely boggy, so stay tight into the wall until the road is reached.

6 Cross over the road and cross a moorland pasture, to another gate on a wide track. Pass through on the track and turn immediately right, following the path through the boulders to the top of Gutter Tor. Compared to Sheeps Tor, this is a short, sharp scratch of a climb.

7 Continue to climb up, past the rocky outcrop to a stile in the fence and then on to the summit trig point. Now, this is where the fast running starts as it is nearly all downhill from here. A couple of paths now carry straight on from the summit, but out of the two obvious ones, take the right one as it descends easily towards Ringmoor Cottage, by a small plantation. The track dips and the trees disappear out of view temporarily, but after a short climb reappear. At the left edge of the trees is a stile over on to a road.

8 Cross straight over the road, to pick up a grassy path, which soon becomes a rocky gully through gorse bushes. The track follows the line of a wall on the right, before coming out on to a farm track. Turn left and follow a short way to a road.

9 Turn right to cross the cattle grid and descend quickly to the ford. You can follow the road over the bridge, but the ford is the race route and much more fun. Back on the road, climb up to the T-junction visited before and turn left, past the school and back to the finish by the pub.

Devonport Leat

13 Princetown and the Aqueduct

Distance	11.8Km (7.4 miles)
Ascent	137m (450ft)
Grade	T2b
Start / Finish	Princetown visitor centre SX 590 734 (50.5441 -3.9909)

An easy to follow route on a foul weather day, from the main, central hub of Princetown. Based around HMP Dartmoor, a 19th century prison, which at 1,430ft above sea level, is the highest settlement on the moor. Complete with cafés, traditional pubs and the Dartmoor National Park visitors centre, Princetown is an ideal starting place for many adventures.

While the route visits only two tors, it is steeped in history, taking in an ancient stone cross, one of many scattered across the moor, dating back to at least 1240. It also follows a man-made, granite leat, constructed in 1790 to take water 27 miles across the moor to the Plymouth dock, and finishes along the remains of the old Princetown and Dartmoor Railway, last used in 1956.

Upon return we recommend having a mooch around the churchyard, which along with the prison, was built by the Napoleonic prisoners of war once they had trudged up from the naval base in Plymouth. Some of the builders were buried in the churchyard and are visited from time to time by their relatives.

The breakfasts are hearty at the Fox Tor Café, the local 'Jail Ale' brewed 100m from the town centre, is best sampled at the Prince of Wales Inn, and if coffee is your bag, head over to the Dewerstone store for a rich brew. For the ill-equipped, there is also an outdoor gear shop called Ice Warrior in the same street.

13 Princetown and the Aqueduct

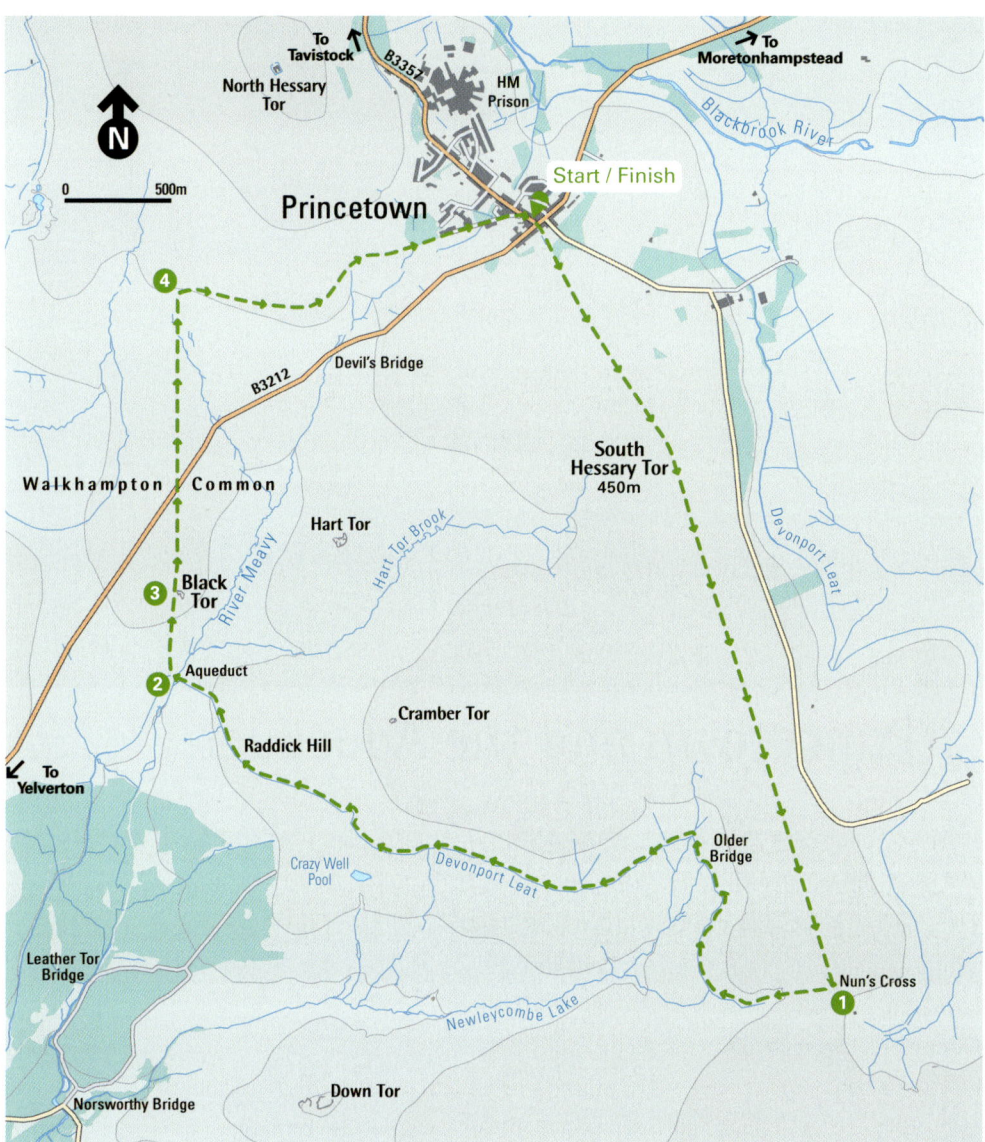

Route

From the High Moorland Visitor Centre steps, follow the wide stony track gently uphill, past South Hessary Tor, pausing only to look back at unnerving views of the category C prison, and then run on to Nun's Cross Farm. A 90-degree right turn takes you past the stone cross and on to the leat. Follow this all the way to an aqueduct, which once crossed, you climb up to Black Tor with stunning views to the south over Plymouth Sound. Cross the road and make your way over open moorland towards the telegraph mast on North Hessary Tor, before returning to the start along the wide, disused railway track.

Princetown and the Aqueduct 13

North Hessary from Black Tor

Detailed directions

START At the mini roundabout outside the visitor centre, look for the track to the right which goes to the left of the Plume of Feathers Inn. Pass through the gate and follow the stone track uphill. Passing through a second gate takes you on to open moorland but still on a well-trodden / cycled stone track. The going is easy as you pass South Hessary Tor on the left, and numerous tracks begin to appear on both sides. Ignore these and carry straight on as it descends to a Dartmoor farmhouse. Nun's Cross Farm appears on the left, and the stone Nun's Cross on the right.

Aqueduct

❶ Ignoring the track ahead as it rises uphill in front, instead turn right 90 degrees. There is no clear track here but after only 100 yards or so of grass, a more definite track appears through ruins and a gnarled tree. Stretching out now ahead is the Devonport Leat, a narrow waterway which appears out of a tunnel on the left. Follow the leat now, ignoring all other tracks, as it meanders across open moorland on its way to Burrator Reservoir, which can be seen over to the left, surrounded by forest and flanked by the impressive Sheeps Tor.

Black tor

❷ The leat suddenly quickens as it descends steeply to cross over the River Meavy by way of an aqueduct, and the runner must tread carefully as the rocks are often

Devonport Cascade

13 Princetown and the Aqueduct

Leather Tor in the distance

wet and slippery. Use the aqueduct as a bridge on the wooden boards conveniently provided, and then leave the leat and turn right to climb the tor ahead, following the paths and low, stone farm walls.

❸ At the tor, called Black Tor, bear half-right aiming for the large telegraph tower to the north-west, even in infamous Dartmoor mist, the red lights can still be visible to aid navigation. If in doubt, follow the sound of cars on the main Princetown to Plymouth road, and upon reaching said road cross and keep heading uphill. There is a myriad of trods and paths all making their way towards the popular cycle track, formerly the railway line. If you are unlucky, you might cross a spring and if you have not already, you may well get wet feet within a mile of the finish.

❹ Upon reaching the railway, turn right and follow it back to the visitor centre via an old railway building and Princetown fire station.

14 Princetown to Burrator and Back

King's Tor at dawn – SW

Distance	25.6km (16 miles)
Ascent	410m (1,344ft)
Grade	T3a
Start / Finish	Princetown visitor centre SX 590 734 (50.5441 -3.9909)

For those who want a longer run but don't want to think too much, this run gives you a long trail run on good trails, with very little chance of getting lost (famous last words). Starting and finishing from the same point, there is the option of cutting this short by taking the right turning at Nun's Cross Farm as per the previous, shorter route.

Route

Head south from the town following a broad track all the way down to a small bridge by Gutter Tor Refuge, which lies encircled in trees. Head up the tor in front and across open moorland, then paths and lanes to the village of Meavy via a ford. Turn right and head to Burrator Dam on paths. Head up left to find the leat, turn right and follow, bearing left to cross a footbridge. Follow this broad, old railway line back to Princetown.

14 Princetown to Burrator and Back

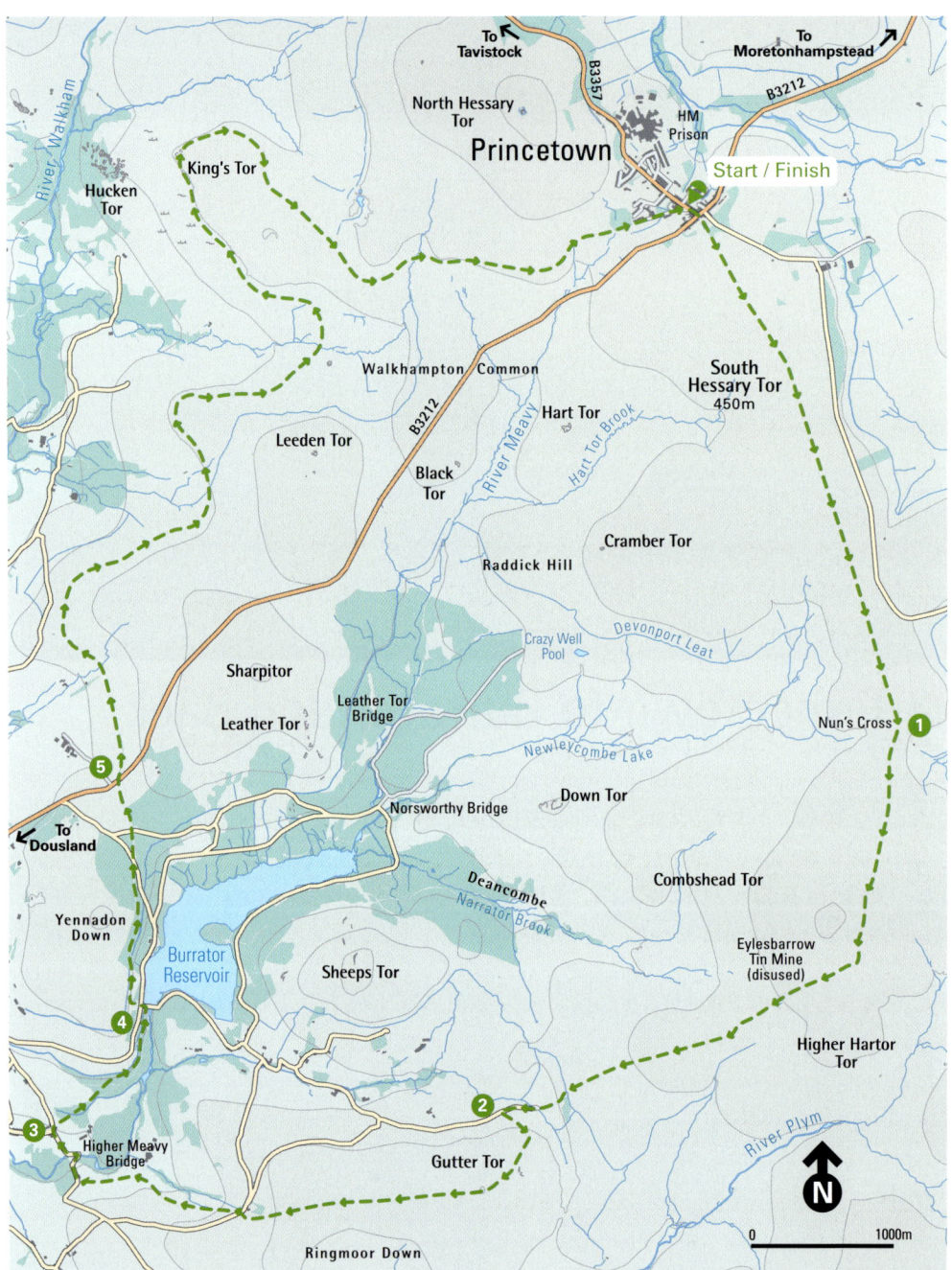

Detailed directions

START At the mini roundabout outside the visitor centre look for the track to the right, which goes to the left of the Plume of Feathers Inn. Pass through the gate and follow the stone track uphill. Passing through a second gate takes you on to open moorland but still on a well-trodden / cycled stone track. The

Princetown to Burrator and Back 14

Burrator Reservoir – SW

going is easy as you pass South Hessary Tor on the left, and numerous tracks begin to appear on both sides. Ignore these and carry straight on as it descends to a Dartmoor farmhouse, Nun's Cross Farm appears on the left and the stone-built Nun's Cross on the right.

❶ Carry straight on uphill, still on the main track. The navigation and route-finding is easy. The track crests the hill, and with ruins on the right and left, stay straight on and follow this track ignoring all others all the way down until a small building, surrounded by evergreen trees, is seen on your left. This is Gutter Tor Refuge and is a type of hostel owned by the MOD.

❷ Cross the bridge directly ahead and follow the track / road, until a wide track comes in on the left. Turn left here and follow to a gate. At the gate, turn right, uphill, along the fence line to the tor at the top called Gutter Tor. Go through the rocky outcrops and then cross the stile in the fence, and run to the trig point. From here, take the middle track, initially downhill, to the left-hand corner of a plantation. Cross the stile and go over the road. Go straight ahead and down a rough, stony track to a lane, where you turn left to meet a road. Turn right, down across the cattle grid, and down through the ford. (You can use the bridge to the right if you like to keep your feet dry)

❸ Climb the hill on the road ahead towards the village of Meavy. At the left turning into the village, carry

Plantations surround Burrator. – SW

Ingra Tor – SW

14 Princetown to Burrator and Back

A logan stone – one that moves. – SW.

straight on and after the first building on the right, turn right through the gate on a waymarked footpath. Follow through the field and a few gates, before climbing the left fork up through the trees to meet a dry leat. The path follows the leat to a wide track junction. Head left again uphill to meet the road by a public toilet. Turn right and follow the road to the dam.

❹ With the dam on the right, and a road going ahead and then round to the right, turn left to climb a faint footpath up the steep bank for a short sharp stretch. On meeting the leat at the top, turn right and follow this on easy ground. Take the left fork away from the leat on a footpath, formerly the old railway line, and climb gently up the hill to cross a bridge over a minor road. Carry straight on and cross another road to meet a forest. Turn left on the path with the trees on your right and head over a cycle bridge, crossing over a main road.

❺ This is a popular mountain bike track and is easy to follow. It follows the line of the old railway, and climbs gently all the way up to Princetown. You will meander with the contours, past tors, old quarries and under packhorse bridges. Follow all the way back to Princetown and the start.

North East

The north-eastern part of Dartmoor is traversed by a series of geological fault lines, lying generally from north-west to south-east, and creating deep valleys. These make for great trail running, and although there is some open moorland to run over, the feeling on this side of the moor is much softer, and less wild than, say, the North West. Yet, while there are few peaks much over 500 metres in height, the steep-sided valleys make for some interesting elevation statistics on the routes.

Bonehill Rocks (Route 17) – SW

Hookney Tor (Route 16) – SW

Castle Drogo high above the valley

15 Fingle Bridge and Castle Drogo

Distance	8km (5 miles)
Ascent	190m (620ft)
Grade	T2a
Start / Finish	Fingle Bridge Inn SX 743 899 (50.6956 -3.7805)

The River Teign is one of the main rivers to flow off the moor and out to sea. As with most rivers, they are obvious honeypots for towns and village settlements, even castles. More importantly, from our perspective, there are some great valley trails to run along.

This route has all that you would want from a valley trail run: a high cliff top path, a riverside trail, a couple of Dartmoor tors, a castle and finally a pub. The tors, Sharp and Hunter's offer great views of the valley and are extremely easy to access, vertigo notwithstanding. The Fingle Bridge Inn is at the start and finish of the route and sits beside the riverbank. My advice would be to visit after the run.

The run follows a route just below Castle Drogo's lofty position. The building is now owned by the National Trust and has the honour of being England's youngest castle, having been finally completed in 1930. Obviously, this was not built as a defensive structure, more of a country house. In the last few years, the building has had to undergo a major refurbishment at great cost, with the National Trust launching a public appeal to help raise the funds. Unfortunately, the design of its medieval-style, flat roof, exposed to the typical Dartmoor weather of almost constant rain, wind, and temperature fluctuations, meant that the building leaked before it was finished. Water also penetrated the masonry around the windows and

15 Fingle Bridge and Castle Drogo

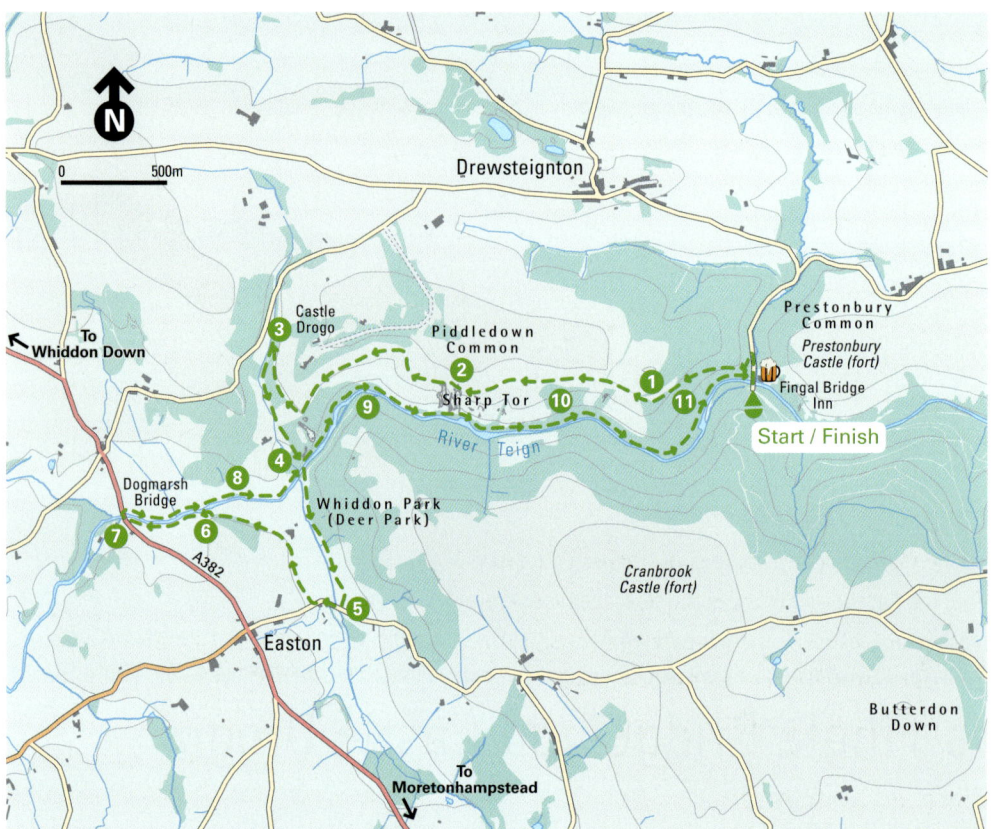

between the granite blocks, the client's insistence that the windows had no sills, reminiscent of medieval design, had not really helped the matter. That said, the building is still an impressive structure and all its treasured contents are slowly being re-displayed.

The route itself is not technical in any way, and a standard trail shoe will suffice as the run follows good paths which are frequently trodden. The valley itself is sheltered, but as the route stays high for the first couple of miles, dress according to conditions, as it can get quite wet and wild. Hey, it's Dartmoor!

If you are a National Trust member, it makes sense to park at Castle Drogo, as the site has a café, toilets and lots of parking. However, to park free as a non-member, I would park in the lay-bys provided on the side of the road just up from the Fingle Bridge Inn, and this is where the route starts.

To get to the start, follow signs to Drewsteignton, and then Fingle Bridge, parking on the left before the bridge and inn. For those who do park by the castle, head south from the car park, and pick up the route from there, by turning right once on the path high above the river valley.

Route

From the inn, head up the access road and take the first path on the left up a steep hill. Follow to the end of the valley and under the castle. At the road, turn left and follow the footpath signs to the bridge by the river. Cross the bridge and turn right along a track, to a gate on to a road. Turn right and right again

Fingle Bridge and Castle Drogo 15

Fingle Bridge, River Teign

at the footpath and follow the river bank to the road. Turn right at the end, over the bridge, then immediately right again to follow the opposite river bank. Follow the path back to the previous footbridge and then the riverbank back to the packhorse bridge by the inn.

Detailed directions

START Start at the ancient packhorse bridge, with the inn on your right, resisting the temptation of its food and ale. Head up the road for 120 metres and then turn left on a path as a wooden fence comes down to meet the road. This is a steep climb, and the only real one on the route. It is runnable, fitness level dependant, but is criss-crossed with roots and stones, so watch your footing.

1 The slope eases after two thirds of a mile, and the path emerges from the trees to give great views of the Teign valley to the west. A path comes in from the right, but stay straight on to a gate, and pass through it. The path is easy now and flat, so get your head up and enjoy the view ahead.

2 Ignore another path coming in from the right and stay on the path, signposted Hunter's Path, to reach Sharp Tor via a couple of bends. Feel free to scramble up and look down the valley if you like heights, and

Steep Valley near Sharp Tor

Easy trails

Footbridge over the Teign

15 Fingle Bridge and Castle Drogo

then keep heading west on the path again, now with the first glimpses of Castle Drogo high on the hillside in front.

3 Numerous paths from the castle now come down to meet the main path but ignore these, and follow signs for Dogmarsh Bridge. The high valley path now comes to an end at Hunter's Tor, the viewpoint, marked by a signpost, is worth a visit if you are not in any rush. Back on the main path, take the hairpin right and descend quickly to a gate and a junction with a road. Turn left to follow the road downhill to a cattle grid.

4 Cross over the cattle grid, where there is a gate on the right, and bear left following the footpath signs. These take you down a trail to the left of a cottage and gardens called Coombe, and it is simply divine. The path comes out at the river by a footbridge, and you now have three options to deviate from the guide. Turn left, and you head straight back for just shy of two miles to the start. Alternatively, cross over the bridge and turn left again to get to the same location, on a slightly easier path. To get the full benefit of the route, I recommend crossing the bridge, and turn right after the steps to follow a broad permissive track.

5 Assuming you took my advice, follow the track through an open meadow, past a farm with a sign saying *'Private. No public Access'* and make your way to a large gate which opens out on to a lane.

6 Turn right over a bridge and then right on to another footpath opposite a house. Run through the field to the same, previous 'private' farm and then on to a track which enters a woodland. At the end of the wood, follow the path right and down some steps to the riverbank again.

7 Turn left and run across the meadow by the side of the river and cross a stile on to the road. Take care as this can be a busy road, and turn right across the Dogmarsh Bridge, immediately turning right again, back on to the path on the other side of the river.

8 Follow the riverbank along a good vehicle-sized track to a gate, and then on again and back to the footbridge you crossed earlier.

9 Staying on this side of the river, to my mind, is a much more enjoyable run than the broad track on the other side, carry straight on under the steep hillside on which Castle Drogo sits.

10 The river now meanders, and the path follows accordingly. Pass through gates, designed to keep horses in and out of certain areas, and stay on the well-trodden path. At one point, the path climbs a steep rocky section, complete with bannister to help on the man-made steps. Watch your step here, as the stone is polished and treacherous in the wet.

11 The brief climb is short and quickly descends again, back to the riverbank and continues through the trees to a gate by the bridge marking the end, and more importantly the inn.

A Pilgrimage to Jay's Grave 16

Grimspound at dawn – SW

16 A Pilgrimage to Jay's Grave

Distance	13.6km (8.51 miles)
Ascent	383m (1,258ft)
Grade	T2a
Start / Finish	Hound Tor car park SX 739 792 (50.5990 -3.7823)

A fine run, taking in a good mix of woodland tracks, farm paths and open moorland, with limited exposure to the elements. Ideal in all but the worst weather conditions. Trail shoes will be sufficient, rather than studded fell shoes.

The route starts from a free car park, popular at weekends so get there early to secure a spot. The nearest town is Bovey Tracy which is off down to the south-east, but there are no facilities at the start or on the route, so stock up on provisions if required before setting off.

Jay's Grave is the first point of interest on the run, and one which is legendary and thus popular with tourists. As with Stephen's Grave on the west side of the moor, romantic tragedy is at the heart of the story. Young servant maid, meets wealthy landowner's son, they discuss the birds and the bees, and then act out the practical. Maid gets pregnant, son gets cold feet due to his position and standing, girl takes her own life. As per the nature of her death in strictly religious times, she was buried on the boundaries of the local parishes, and not buried in consecrated grounds. Hence her position by a road / track junction. The grave is well-maintained and fresh flowers are laid every day. This is part of its charm and mystery. Local folk singer of international fame, Seth Lakeman, based one of his best known songs 'Kitty Jay' on the tale.

16 A Pilgrimage to Jay's Grave

Further along the route, after farms and old mine workings, you get an almost birds-eye view of Grimspound from Hookney Tor. A Bronze Age settlement, consisting of a perimeter wall around a set of hut circles. It's an interesting site, and well-maintained by English Heritage. If you are not chasing a fast time, linger and explore before moving on.

Coming into the 20th Century, further along the route is a WW2 memorial to the site of an RAF plane crash. Members of 49 Squadron, flying a bomber back from a raid in 1941, crashed here when the pilot became disorientated in the typical Dartmoor fog. Ironically, the hill above, Hamel Down, was identified as a site where enemy gliders might land in an invasion attempt, so large, wooden poles were erected to prevent, or more likely hinder, any attempt. Some of these remain today.

A Pilgrimage to Jay's Grave   16

Haytor in the distant mist – SW

Route

From the car park at the western base of Hound Tor, head north on the road to a gate, and turn left across two fields to reach a road and Jay's Grave. Cross over behind the grave and follow the path to another road. Cross over to a gate and turn right to head north. Follow the path through farmland before turning left and uphill to Hookney Tor. Descend south to the valley, then turn left to follow a path past a memorial, then back down to pick up the same, previous path back to the car park.

Detailed directions

START Come out of the car park on its right side, while facing up the slope to Hound Tor, and turn immediately right and right again on a road. The road ahead splits, take the right fork. This lane is rarely used, mainly due to a gate, so is relatively traffic-free if you don't count the odd tractor.

❶ Without passing through the gate at the end, turn left to pass through another gate, to find a path which climbs steadily through a field. Head left away from the wall on your right slightly to make for a gate in the wall ahead. Carry straight on this public footpath to cross through another gate closer this time to the wall.

❷ Heading downhill now, handrail the boundary on the right to a gate which brings you out on to a lane, directly opposite Jay's Grave, unmistakeable as it guards the entrance to your way ahead.

Bridle path, Jay's Grave route

Ancient roads and ancient homes – SW

A Pilgrimage to Jay's Grave

3 Follow the path directly behind the grave, through a gate to run on a good track which climbs alongside a woodland on the right. The path peaks briefly then descend quickly to another road, accessed by a gate. Bear left here and immediately right to cross the road and pass through a large, wooden gate, marked with a fingerpost. Remember this gate, as you will pass back through this on the return leg.

4 Once through the gate, turn right to access a smaller gate and stile which enters into Heathercombe woodlands on the Mariner's Way. The estate woodland is well-maintained here, as is the path, which is well-marked by the yellow public footpath arrows. Follow these along fast trails to Heathercombe Farm and a path junction.

5 Head straight on through the farm and a gate ahead, and then follow to another gate. After this second one, bear right, staying on the waymarked path as before, through managed woodland. A large, wooden stile marks the end of the estate woodland, and the terrain now changes to pastureland.

6 Go straight ahead though a field to another boundary, and then across a wide field to a stile in the hedgerow, to the right of the farm on the left. The path crosses the farm drive to another stile and then more lush pastureland.

7 The ground gently drops away now, and slightly right, to make its way to another field by way of a stile. The way is obvious, and there are no other paths to turn on to at this stage. Cross a stream and then on to more marshy ground. Here, look out for a water trough as the path turns left to gain a wide, vehicle track leading to another farm at Lower Hookner.

8 The path is well-marked and stays to the left of the main, farm buildings to emerge on to a farm track. Turn left here, and then at the first gate, not 5 metres ahead on the right, turn right to pass through it. Once through, turn left to follow the direction of the slightly obscured wooden fingerpost, to handrail the hedge on the left.

9 The path follows a small brook, so expect a little moisture and mud. Cross three more fields, keeping to the path to cross a stile and granite bridge, to enter another working farm. Watch out for the protective geese here, and numerous chickens. Keep to the right of the main farmhouse, and then turn immediately left. The main path carries straight on, but ignore this and head up and left to a gate with a wooden sign saying *"Bridlepath"* on the wall next to it.

10 Once through the gate, obey the sign ahead which proclaims; *"Dangerous Mineshafts, please keep to the Bridlepath"*. Head straight on up, following the line of a stream on the right. I can't dress this up, it's a steep pull for almost a mile, but you can curse all you like, as all will be forgiven once at the top, honest!

11 The path is fairly straightforward to follow and passes a small reservoir over to the left. Go through an ancient, boundary embankment, and then head up to the wall ahead. A wooden gate is your target, upon the reverse is the same warning as at the bottom of the hill just climbed. Presuming you avoided the mineshafts, once through the gate, turn hard left to follow the wall, still climbing, but easier now. Cross a low boundary wall and head slightly left to the rocky outcrop of Hookney Tor. The 360° views of the western moor are now great, and to quote a famous Aussie beer advertisement of the 90s: *"Eh Snowy, I can see the pub from here!"* The pub in question is the white building, due east of the tor and called the Warren House Inn, the third highest pub in England.

16 A Pilgrimage to Jay's Grave

Upper Webburn – SW

12 Unfortunately for yourselves and Snowy, you aren't going that way, so instead, turn left and head steeply downhill on a thin track to the obvious stone ring known as Grimspound. Head around to the left in a clockwise direction to reach a main track heading off, left. This track leads into what appears to be the main entrance of the Grimspound settlement, but instead turns left up the valley.

13 The slope is gentle and after a while comes to a split. Take the right one, which contours around the hillside and swings right. As the path flattens out through the heather, a memorial comes into view on the right, with the inscription on the far side.

14 Return to the main path, now downhill, and head for the right corner of the woodland. The path is obvious, and the running is excellent. A nice reward after the previous, stiff climb. The path swings right at the edge of the woodland boundary, and then returns to the gate by the road, previously crossed, before entering the woods on your left.

15 Cross the road, to retrace your steps up and over the shallow hill to make your way back to Jay's Grave. However, this time, once at the road, turn right and follow the road back towards Hound Tor and the car park below it.

Far from the Madding Crowd – Haytor

Hound Tor – MB

17 Far from the Madding Crowd – Haytor

Distance	13.6km (8.5 miles)
Ascent	457m (1,500ft)
Grade	F2
Start / Finish	Haytor lower car park SX 765 771 (50.5808 -3.7452)

This route is designed to keep us 'far from the madding crowd' apart from the start and finish. Due to its relative proximity to the large towns of Newton Abbot, Paignton, and Torquay, Haytor is a popular honey-pot upon which many locals and tourists descend. The large, hay-bale shaped structure can be seen from the towns mentioned and is an easy tor to visit due to the very convenient, three, small car parks situated on the road, just an ice creams throw from the tor itself. For that reason, it is often swarming with folk. Some people park at the bottom car park, by the visitor centre and toilets if they can, the car park being small, and in doing so have the furthest to walk to visit the rock itself. Others park at the top of the hill, giving themselves the easiest of climbs but no loo. Often, in the dryer weather, the middle car park, on grass, is useable and this gives a not too far, not too short pull to the attraction.

Haytor itself is indeed an impressive tor, standing taller off the ground than many. It offers a range of good climbs for enthusiasts on one face, but be prepared for an audience. The opposite side can be climbed with ease, facilitated by steps having been cut into the rock itself to allow Queen Victoria to take in the view from the flat summit. There was even talk this century of a type of stairlift or escalator up the same side, to allow those with disability to also take in the marginally better view of the surrounding moorland and

17 Far from the Madding Crowd – Haytor

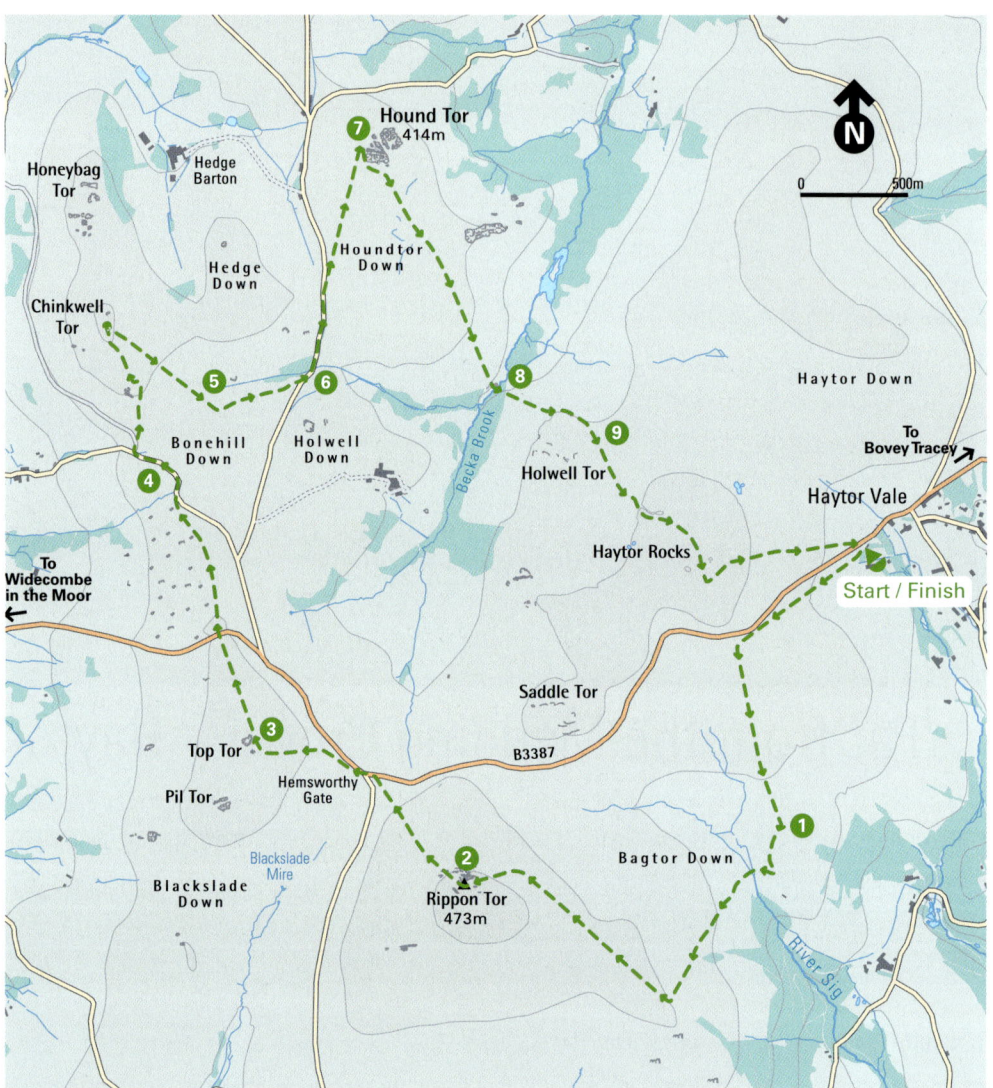

coast, than from the base of the rock. Hey, Snowdon has a train station on the top! Arguably, adjacent to Haytor Rocks, Haytor Lowman is more impressive, particularly from the south-western side.

All that being said, many of the surrounding tors are also worth a visit and typically, due to their distance from the road, less crowded. Nonetheless, this run will finish by running past the famous Haytor, and no running guidebook, would be complete without visiting it.

The Dartmoor National Park visitor centre at the base of Haytor has a loo, and often an ice cream van, so it makes sense to park here if possible. If it is full, then by all means start from any of the others, which the first half mile of the route passes through in any case.

This side of the moor is much tamer, and the feel is softer. The ground is firmer, and the lack of 'long grass' makes for a different environment. Some may argue that this makes for better running, and for the most part it does. However, as delightful as this route is, it is not typical of much of the rest of Dartmoor.

Far from the Madding Crowd – Haytor

Most of those that I have led and guided over this route come away having experienced great views, runnable climbs, and exhilarating descents. It gives them an appetite for more.

The route is designed to leave the masses behind, only returning to their claustrophobic throng upon reaching the finish. However, leading up to this point you will have run past quarries, from which stone was transported to London to build the bridge of the same name. The granite tracks, built solely for the purpose of transporting these fashioned stones down to the Teign Estuary and on to barges, still remain, and this route follows some of them. It is a run of exploration and numerous other tors are detailed in the route description.

The well-stocked town of Bovey Tracy, back down the hill, is a good place to get a pre-run breakfast or snacks for the run. For afters, I recommend the Rugglestone Inn for a pint and a feed, over the other side by the village of Widdicombe in the Moor.

Note: the car parks charge for their use so you should come prepared.

Haytor from Bonehill Rocks – MB

Running past Haytor – MB

Route

Head uphill on the left of the road to pass Bag Tor and then climb up to Rippon Tor. Cross the valley to the west, to then climb to Top Tor. Turn right to pass through three more tors, before heading north over to Hound Tor. Turn south-east to head over to Haytor via Greystone Rocks, and Holwell Quarry. Finish by descending the hill back to the car park.

Detailed directions

START From the bottom-most car park, head up the grassy slope on the left-hand side of the road. This takes you through the middle car park before the slope steepens to crest at the top car park. At the far end of the top car park, turn left to follow a trod, with Haytor directly behind you. The way weaves though gorse and low shrubs and gradually downhill to a gate in the corner of a wall. Pass through and carry straight on to Bag Tor.

1 Turn ninety degrees right to face south west and follow a now wider track, which leads down to a low ford through a river. Follow the track uphill, following the line of the wall on the left to a gate at the top

17 Far from the Madding Crowd – Haytor

corner. Without crossing, turn right to stay on this side of the wall and follow it, contouring around the hill. Rippon Tor now appears up the slope to the left, and upon coming across a gateway, pass through and climb to the summit trig point, which lies inside a stone, circular shelter.

2 A path leads off the summit to the right of the original approach direction, and this leads down to a gate by a road junction. The run down here is one of the many fast descents on this route, so fill your boots. Pass through the gate and over the cattle grid. Ignoring the road off to the left, instead spy a path between the two roads ahead, on open moorland just beyond a small roadside car park. Take this to climb easily up to Top Tor.

3 Prepare for another fast descent, and turn right to head north down an easy gradient on a good path. Cross the road, opposite another car park, and continue on the path downhill to yet another small car park by a stream, where Bonehill Rocks lie on the far side. Popular with boulderers, Bonehill Rocks is, in essence, just that, a pile of rocks. Go up the steep but short section, skirt round to the right of the main concentration of rocks and descend again to a road, where you turn left.

4 At the boundary crossing, after only a noticeably short time, turn right over a stream, and follow a bridleway initially, before taking the right trod up a steep hill to the next tor, which is called Bell Tor. Go through this tor, and still uphill again to the next one, Chinkwell Tor. From the top of this, turn right and descend via a small tree on a faint trod, down towards a wall. There is now some tricky route-finding. Bear in mind, we do this for fun.

5 If you get all the way to the wall, turn right and follow … and again as it bends ninety degrees left. This, however, can be a bit boggy so if you happen to find the trod off the top of Chinkwell Tor, which curves right and then left, some fifty metres away from the wall, the way will be somewhat drier. Not dry, but definitely drier. Hey, this is Dartmoor.

6 Whichever way you go, you end up at a road, where you turn left and follow over a cattle grid and uphill. At the top, the boundary on the right ends, so bear right across open moor along a trod towards the mass of Hound Tor ahead.

7 At the tor, turn right and keep to the high ground following a path over to a stile over a wall. Go through this to access open pasture, with horse jumps scattered about. Keep left and pick up the path off to the left, which descends quickly to a gate then a stream. Use either the bridge or ford to cross.

8 Climb up the other side, over large boulders and climb across to a steeper climb again below Holwell Tor. The path levels off on the old, stone quarry tramway. Turn left here to follow as it contours around the tor, eventually swinging right. At the Y-shaped junction, take the right path directly uphill and Haytor Rocks come into view.

9 Follow the faint trod, all paths seem to lead now to the famous rock, and climb steadily, aiming for the left-hand outcrop. Pass between the two major outcrops at the top, and then swing left for the obligatory, fast finish to the car park at the bottom.

Moretonhampstead Loop 18

Giant's Grave

18 Moretonhampstead Loop

Distance	14.4km (9 miles)
Ascent	414m (1,538ft)
Grade	T2a
Start / Finish	Tourist information centre SX 753 861 (50.6608 -3.7653)

The town of Moretonhampstead has everything you need as a base for a run: cafés, pubs, a deli, a small supermarket, public conveniences and a couple of car parks. The car parks do charge, but the fee is reduced to £1 on Sundays.

This part of the moor is more farmed than, say, the wild north or barren south moor, and as such, the paths are well marked, generally very runnable. There is far less access land here (i.e., giving you the right to roam) but this does mean there is equally less chance of getting lost.

This particular route is a favourite of mine in poor weather, as despite one high, open spot early on, the route is relatively sheltered by woodland, deep bridleways and generally, gentler terrain.

As the route follows a mix of woodland tracks, bridleways and lanes, trail shoes are sufficient. There are no loos or shops on the way once out of town so, as ever, run prepared.

On the run, look out for the Bronze Age stone circle known as Giant's Grave, where legend has it that Maximajor, the local giant, was buried on the site where he died, being too large and heavy to move. However, sometime after his burial, he was found to have pushed aside the stones and made off, never to be seen again. The legend says that the standing stone, not previously there, was the giant himself, turned

18 Moretonhampstead Loop

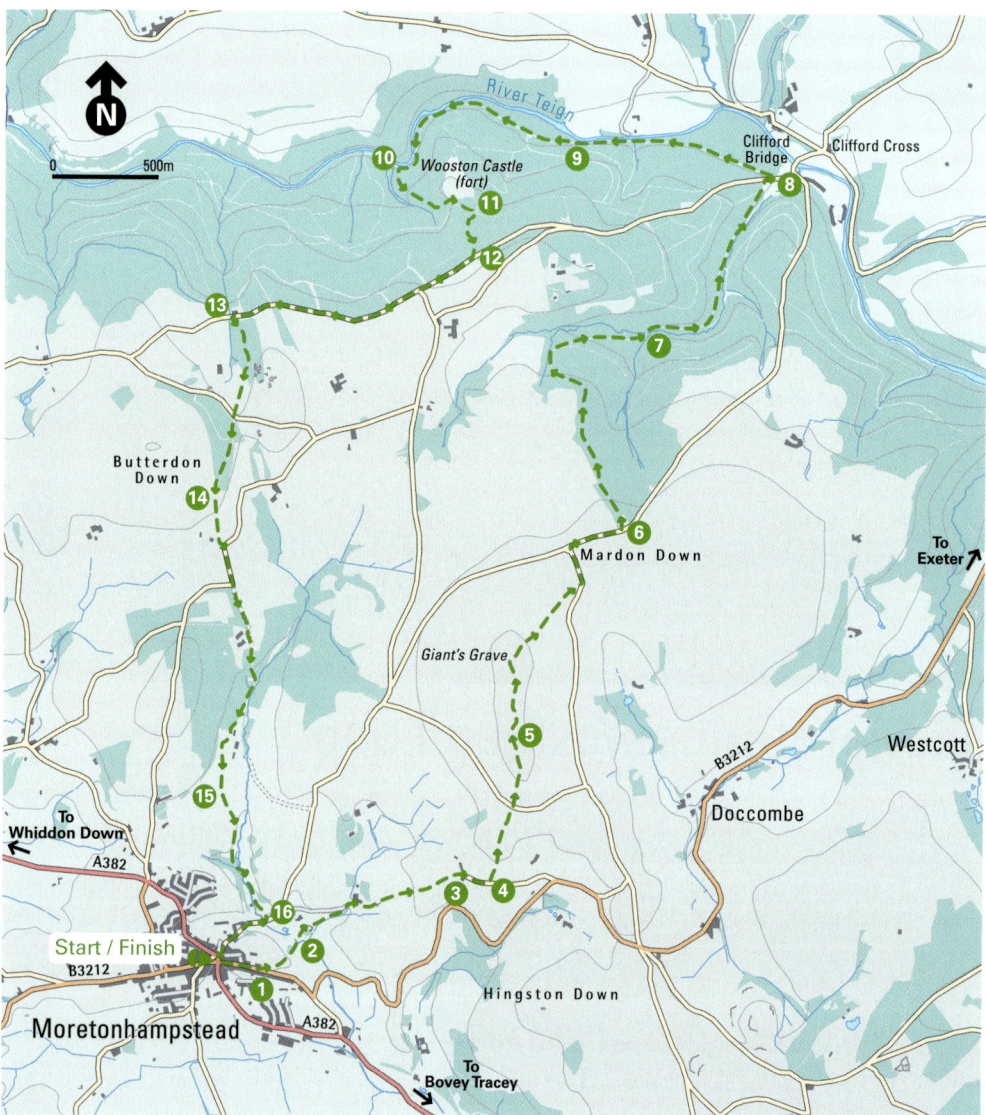

into stone by some kind of spell. The remains of such a miracle can be seen today, as can the standing stone, or menhir just down the hill, formerly known as the Maximajor stone, now called the Headless Cross. The route also takes you into Fingle Woods, jointly run by the National Trust and Woodland Trust, high on the banks above the River Teign. The trails here are well-maintained and great to run on.
Some of the route follows narrow lanes, which although low in traffic are still used by vehicles, so take care.

Route

Head out east from the town centre and up to Mardon Down via paths and tracks. Turn left and north to drop down into the Teign Valley above Clifford Bridge and turn left to follow the river upstream. Turn left again for Wooston Castle, up the valley side to leave the river, and follow paths back to the start.

Moretonhampstead Loop 18

Detailed directions

START From either car park, make for the centre of town and the information centre, located on New Street. Outside, opposite the centre, is a small triangle with benches to sit on and watch the world go by. Facing the White Hart Inn, adjacent to the triangle, turn left and east on the road to a crossroads. Head straight over on Cross Street, past a café and continue on to the end of a line of 17th Century Jacobean alms houses on the left, now owned by the National Trust.

1 A footpath is signed over a stile, on the left at the end of the buildings, and runs across a field containing a children's playpark on the left. Go straight over to a gate, and then following the path down the hillside as it swings left. This is an obvious path, sunken into the earth by the feet of many a traveller.

2 At the bottom, go straight over through a gate, and over the stream on a good path between buildings. The path is well signposted around the gardens and outhouses, climbing steadily. Turn right after the gate on a bridleway. After a short distance, the path is directed off to the left of the main track – follow signs to Yarningdale.

High summer bracken

3 The path comes out at a junction, but carry straight on, ignoring a return path over to the right. The track turns into tarmac here, but still climbs uphill between holiday accommodation and bed and breakfast properties.

4 At the brow of the hill, look out for a footpath on the left, through a gate. The path still climbs, but the top is not far now. At the top of this path, the way opens up on to open moorland, and up to a road. Cross over and follow the trods upwards to the hill top, to gain a main track heading left and north over the top of the ridge.

Follow the sign

5 Run past the cairns, and eventually to the Giant's Grave. As the hill starts to drop away, swing right down an obvious track towards the standing stone or Headless Cross. A road runs from right to left here so turn left in front of an opening, popular as a parking spot, and then on to a T-junction. Turn right here to follow the road.

6 After no more than a couple of hundred metres, take the opening and path on the left, by a colourful noticeboard, showing the paths and trails of the area. This is the opening for Fingle Woods. Follow the track

Busy Moretonhampstead

down, as it handrails the boundary on the left. The path is in great condition and makes for lovely running, after the initial climb up to Mardon Down. Treasure the memory of this downhill for later!

7 The path swings left and then bends right, still descending. The tracks are now marked by colourful waymarkers and follow these downhill to a junction with a bridge on the left. Turn left here over the bridge, and round to the right, following the main track downhill. The broad path follows a stream on the right.

8 At an obvious concrete bridge, stay left and do not cross. The path climbs gently and only briefly, before descending again to a gate, and a small car park. Go through the car park to the road, and turn right, still downhill. After 100m, a signpost points the way to Fingle Bridge on the left, so turn here on a well-manicured, hard track. If you miss this you hit Clifford Bridge over the River Teign, and you have gone too far, so turn back.

9 Follow this now, above the river valley, upstream, as the track then descends to meet the riverbank. A weir path is an option on the right, which follows a grassy trod, before returning to the main path. If preferred, stay on the main track.

10 After a while, as the path bends left to follow the line of the river, and then right, a wooden signpost points up a steep track to the left, towards 'Wooston Castle'. Remember the downhill now? Turn left up the steep track and keep on to a gate. Go through and reach the top by the ancient earth works of the fortification. To be honest, after such a climb, the castle is not that spectacular, but the views over the valley to the left certainly are.

11 Leaving the fort, follow the signposted path uphill. Ignore the path off to the right, signposted to 'Fingle Bridge', instead carry straight on up the track. Another sign points to 'Hill Fort car park', so follow that and through a gate at the top.

12 At the road, turn right on a quiet lane. The uphill gradient is easy, and the lane soon descends to reach a cottage on the right. Opposite this, on the left is a waymarked footpath, which goes past a garage. Head through the stile and climb steadily up through lush woodland, carpeted by bluebells in the spring.

13 The path leaves the woodland, underneath Willingstone Rock, and crosses a field. Head straight for the telegraph pole in the middle, then straight on to the field corner. The path crosses a road now and goes straight on into another woodland. Here, a Community Interest Company has set up a woodland retreat, but the public footpath is well marked through the settlement.

14 At the end of the path, a stile leads on to a track, so turn left downhill here, between two walls to reach a road. Carry straight on and at the right-hand bend in the road, again stay straight on to descend a bridleway.

15 Here the footpath is clearly marked by public footpath signs, again through woodland and farm pasture, making its way past a farm and to a path junction. Either path takes you back into town, however, the left fork downhill is much more enjoyable. Follow this, signed for 'Lime Street', down to the valley bottom and turn right, to follow the field perimeter and stream.

16 At the footbridge, cross over and turn right to make for a house and then on to the road. Turn right here, on the road, and follow back into town.

19 Hameldown Hammer

Ubiquitous sheep – MB

Distance	21km (13 miles)
Ascent	680m (2,228ft)
Grade	T4b
Start / Finish	Widecombe village green SX 718 768 (50.5768 -3.8116)

Widecombe in the Moor is a great place to start a run, as long as you don't mind an uphill start. The village is chocolate-box pretty with a village green, a couple of pubs, café, gift shop, car park, loo, and ubiquitous ice cream vendor.

The church in the centre is also an impressive building and is often referred to as the Cathedral of the Moor, but the most famous point of interest about this settlement, is the fair.

Widecombe Fair is probably one of the most famous in the area and, although not the biggest, it is made even more famous by the Dartmoor folk song of the same name with the lyrics:

"Old Uncle Tom Cobley and all"

The fair is relatively small in comparison to many on Dartmoor today, probably due to the fact it is held on the second Tuesday in September, and not a weekend. However, the village is none the worse for it and thrives all year-round, particularly in the summer.

As with most villages on Dartmoor, the car parking, while better than most, is limited, so plan ahead and arrive early in the summer. The Café on the Green, close to the car park is a great spot for eats and other delights, and the two pubs: The Old Inn and Rugglestone Inn offer ales and food. The Old Inn is situated

19 Hameldown Hammer

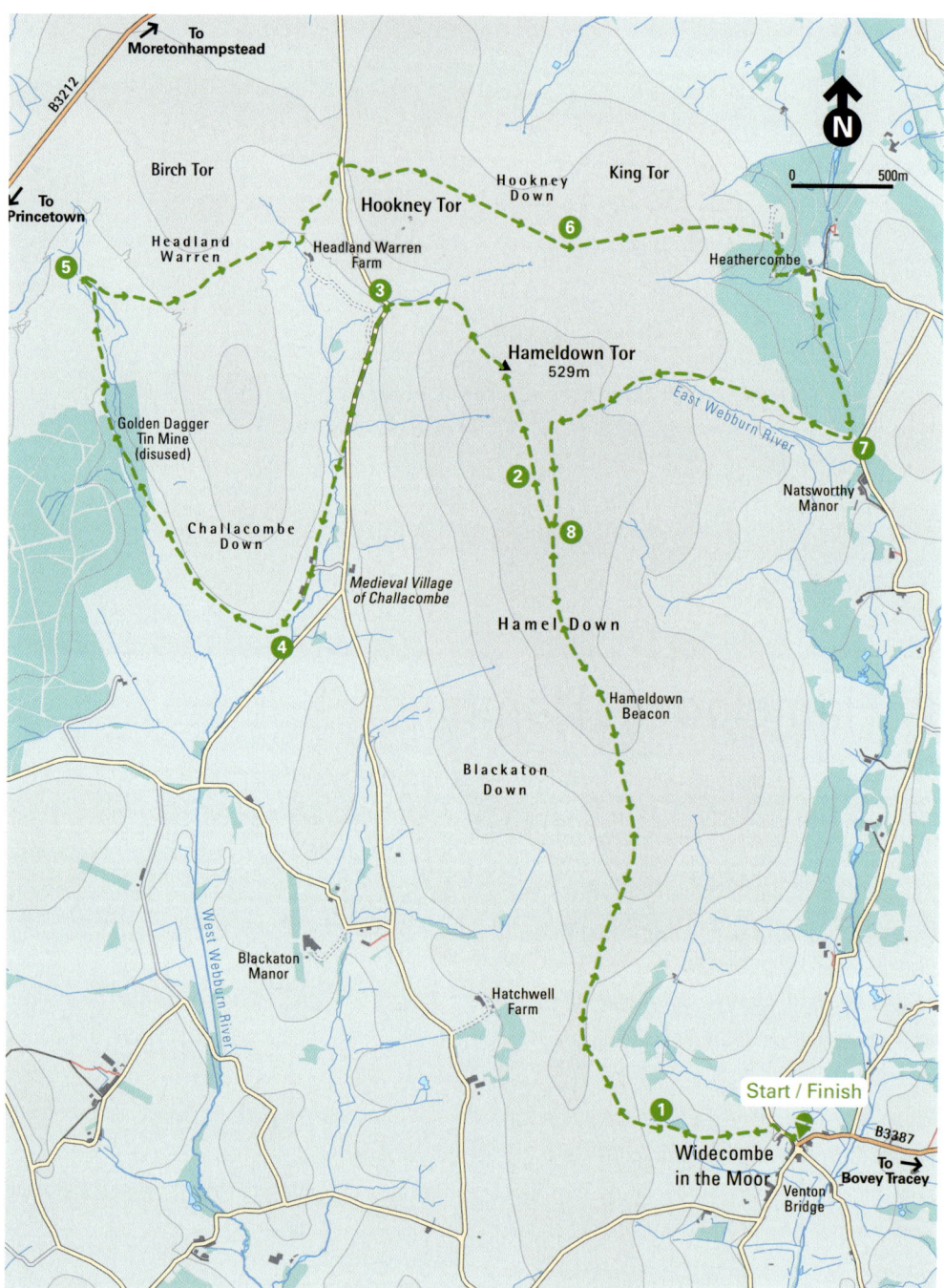

in the centre of the village opposite the church, and has been refurbished to a high standard, while the Rugglestone is a short walk out, past the church on a lane, and is perhaps more rustic and popular with locals.

The run itself takes in a variety of terrain including high, moorland trods, woodland tracks and green lanes, and is now the route of a popular race by a company called Puretrail. On the route you will cross Hameldown

Hameldown Hammer

Beacon, littered with burial cairns, at 532m in height. The Bronze Age settlement of Grimspound, and the Medieval hamlet of Challacombe, complete with Devon longhouses. Their inhabitants shaped this local landscape with cairns and field systems; interesting to acknowledge as you run through them.

This route does involve the double climb of what is a quite exposed ridge, susceptible to the elements, so dress or carry the required kit accordingly. Trail shoes will suffice on this route, although in true, winter conditions, I will personally use studded fell shoes to ensure some fast, downhill running near the end.

Route

Head north out of the village and then left up on to Hamel Down. Continue north to the stone circle, then left to the road and left again through the small hamlet. Turn right to head round, north-west, past a forest on the left. Turn right towards Hookney Tor and then on to join a path heading south through farmland. Turn right and west to regain Hamel Down and head south, retracing your steps back to the start.

Detailed directions

START Standing on the village green, with the church behind you, run out on the road in a northerly direction, with an ice cream kiosk and car park on your right. After approximately 200m, take the first left up a steep lane and climb to the top. The lane becomes a track as it passes a farm but is still runnable.

1 At the gate at the top, go through and turn half right to follow the wall boundary, still climbing. Eventually the path meets another left to right track, so turn right here and keep to the wall boundary on your right. After a slight drop, the path climbs again, straight ahead to the summit ridge of Hameldown Beacon.

2 The main path follows the ridge now, still uphill to the summit cairn and the remains of an old granite cross. Carry straight on to the trig point which is slightly lower than the previous top. From the trig point, head straight down the steep path to the crossroads above the stone circle settlement of Grimspound. Turn left here on the path to meet the road.

3 At the road turn left, still running downhill, and where a stream flows towards the road from the steep hill on the left, take a track on the right though an old field system and pick up a path. Turn left here and follow this through the old, medieval settlement of Challacombe, now a free-range farm.

4 Once through the farm the path starts to bend right, then splits. Take the right fork on a good

Frosty 'babies heads' – MB

19 Hameldown Hammer

track and follow again through a field system until a path re-joins from the right and you meet a wide gate. Go through the gate and follow the wide track through old mine workings to a crossroads by some ruins.

❺ Turn right, uphill, and follow the obvious track, past earth works to a small farm. Take the left fork here away from the farm, still climbing and up to the road. Go straight over the road to follow a path along the side of a low boundary wall. This skirts to the north of Hookney Tor. Feel free to visit the top if you like but stay straight on following the lines of the wall on a track. Don't be tempted to drop to the village, stay high on the hillside.

❻ Carry straight on, under the top of King Tor and then descend towards a treeline. The path then enters into an orchard, and becomes a green lane.

Hamel Down anti-airborne device – MB

Be careful as the descent is steep, and the hard ground can become slippery in the wet. Follow the track to a farm and a crossroads, where you turn right.

❼ Follow this waymarked path through the local estate and all the way to a gate which opens out on to open moorland, with a gate over to your left and a hill to the right. Turn right of course, uphill being our favourite, and follow the track until it meets a fork. Take the left option as it follows the line of the hillside, gently rising as it contours up the hillside, past tall wooden poles, designed to prevent German gliders from landing during the Second World War.

❽ The path eventually leads to the summit of Hameldown again and, at this point, the route retraces your steps back to Widecombe. However, this is now a much faster and more pleasurable run as you can really speed up. Again, be careful on the lane near the end as it can be slippery in the wet.

Lustleigh Cleave – SW

20 The Hobbit Half Marathon

Distance	20.8km (13 miles)
Ascent	768m (2,519ft)
Grade	T4a
Start / Finish	Manaton Church car park SX 749 811 (50.6169 -3.7685)

This side of Dartmoor has a different feel to it compared to the barren, open north moor, and the rugged west side. Instead, this east side is more agricultural, has more villages, and more wooded valleys. Many might see this side of the moor as being tamer, and softer, in terms of shelter from the westerly winds and less exposed to the elements. I would tend to agree, however from a running perspective, this area is to be treated with respect. With its steep valleys and frequent tops it can catch the speedy, flat-road runner off guard. Anyway, who wants to run fast through such lush scenery? I prefer a gentler run in these parts, and regard this route in particular as more of a sightseeing running adventure.

This run begins in the village of Manaton, which along with the rest of the route, drums up images of Tolkien's Shire, where Bilbo Baggins resided. Green fields, well-groomed gardens, immaculate cottages, big and small, and a hearty community for one so small. The village is split in two, the top half accommodating the large, 15th century church, community centre and car park, the lower part is centred around the Kestor Inn. The route starts in the car park which, like many, gets full quickly at weekends in the summer. Some parking can be found on the roadside by the car park, but please park sensibly and refrain from blocking access. Tractors rarely take prisoners. The car park has a fee of £1 for the village church funds.

The Hobbit Half Marathon

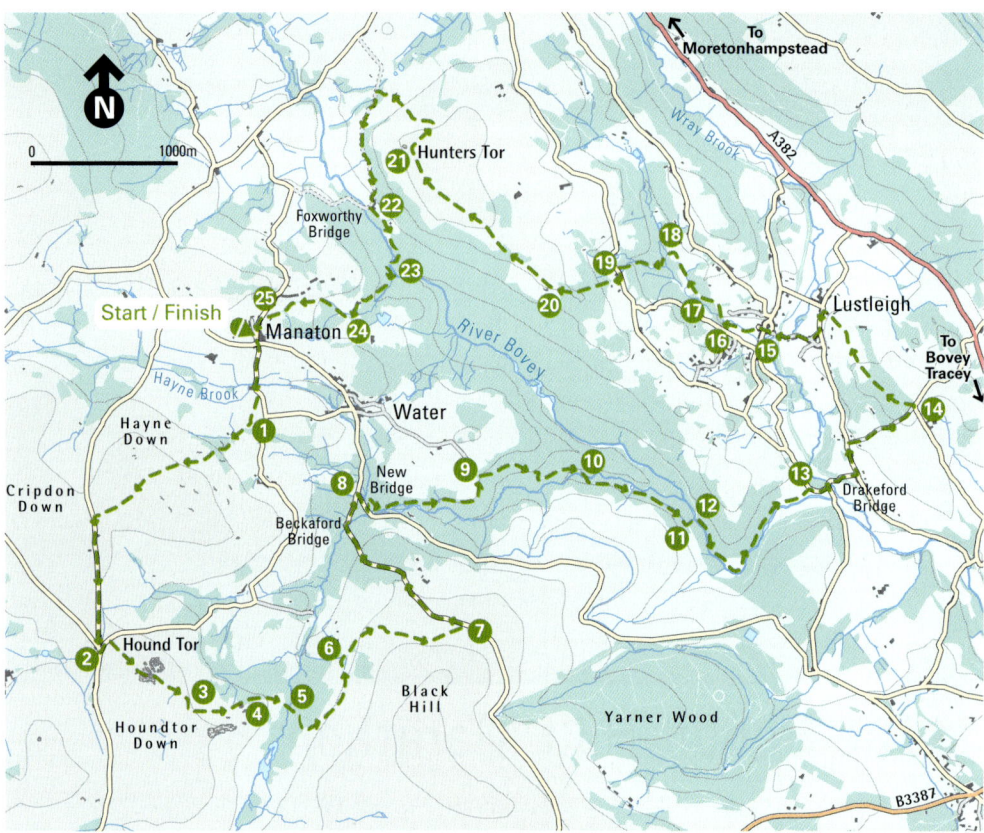

The route visits many key points and features in the area, and while there is a plethora of options to run around here, I believe this particular route offers the best way to see the valley. In the description I will suggest other detours to cut the route short if needed.

Key points of interest on the way include: Bowerman's Nose, Hound Tor and adjacent, 13th century, medieval settlement, Becky Falls, the River Bovey valley, the village of Lustleigh, Sharpitor, Raven's Tor, Hunters Tor and Lustleigh Cleave.

For those taking their time who wish to partake of refreshments, Lustleigh provides a pub, tearoom and small post office / shop (check Sunday opening hours) about two thirds of the way into the run. A public loo is also available here if needed, particularly as there isn't one at the start of the run.

This route, while undulating, is on good tracks and paths with the occasional bits of road to join up the paths, so really aggressive fell shoes are not needed, even in the winter.

Route

Head south out of the village and turn west to Bowerman's Nose. Turn south again to Hound Tor and then east to cross a river. Turn northwards to follow a track to a road and follow left down to another road. Turn right then cross left and head north-east to follow woodland paths and a stream to the River Bovey. Cross the river and follow it downstream to a road. Turn left and follow the road and paths north to Lustleigh.

The Hobbit Half Marathon

Head through the village to make for Sharpitor and north still to Hunters Tor. Turn left to descend west to the river. Cross and return to Manaton up the valley side.

Detailed directions

START Come out of the car park adjacent to the church and turn right to get to the crossroads. Run straight ahead and descend quickly, ignoring the footpath sign on the left. As the road climbs past a house, take the second, large gate on the right, marked with a wooden signpost, to cross a field and obvious path going diagonally across to another gate. Turn right here on a good track and follow to another wooden gate.

1 After passing through the gate, turn hard right and follow the path uphill, now leaving the tress behind and start to climb up towards the crags. (Take the right fork if you wish to climb up to Bowerman's Nose.) At the top, turn left and descend the ridge-line aiming initially for a barn, and then follow the path towards a gate on a road. Turn left and pass through the gate and follow the road.

2 As the road merges with another, turn left to a junction and you will see the mass of Hound Tor ahead, up the slope. Cross the road by the entrance to the car park and climb up the path aiming for the middle of the tor.

3 Hound Tor is split into two big chunks and the gap in between is known as the avenue; use this to pass through and, once beyond, follow the path as it bears right to descend to the right of the ancient village. This is a popular area, so the path is well worn and stays to the right of the settlement to protect its status.

4 The going is good and fast and as the path descends, follow it to the right at first, then aim left towards a rock formation ahead of you, known as Greystone Rocks, and make for a gate at the top of a short rise.

5 Pass through the gate and the path descends steeply down to another gate before reaching a clapper bridge over a stream. Cross over and follow the well-trodden path as it snakes through the woodland. The path is eroded somewhat, and the boulders have been exposed so watch your footing. Dancing feet are a good trait to possess on this ground.

6 The path emerges on to a grassy slope by a wooden fingerpost, and ignoring the temptation to head straight up, follow the signpost pointing left on a flat and easy path. Pass through a gate and downhill to a second gate, after which the path forks. Now is the time to go uphill, so bear right here on a good track, through another gate and continue, following a wall on the left side.

Bowerman's Nose – MB

7 As the wall abruptly turns sharp left, follow it across a grass patch to meet a road. Turn left over the cattle grid and follow the road downhill, over Beckaford Bridge to a T-junction. This can be a busy junction at weekends so take care. Turn right and cross the road, as in approximately 100m, there is a path on the left and you don't want to miss it. Turn here and follow left and then right almost back on yourself. At a crossroads, where the track bears right after no time at all, cross straight over, following the yellow public footpath signs, and not the Becky Falls Trails.

8 The public footpath skirts the upper edge of the river and is criss-crossed with waymarked trails. Stay straight ahead and follow the yellow public footpath signs and you can't go wrong. The path will gradually descend and contour the hillside in a wooded valley. The path can be technical so take care.

9 As the path swings left, it comes out into a clearing and a track junction. A path leads straight on uphill and there are two to the right. Here is a good opportunity to cut the route short and take the uphill path which leads back to Water, and on to Manaton. If staying on course, take the lower track on the right which is a wide forest track, and descend quickly with a few twists and turns.

10 Cross the bridge after the gate over Becka Brook and turn left. This is excellent trail running in a shady forest, and a welcome break from the climbs and technical paths previously encountered. Ignore the first footbridge on the left after 500m but instead take the second, another 500m on, with obvious signposts.

11 The bridge here has some character and an interesting method of stopping vehicles crossing it.

12 On crossing, turn immediately right and take the path through a gate, hugging the River Bovey. More good running along the valley through meadows and trees. In the last meadow, hug the fence line to the left and look for a gate where the fence meets a road. A faint, yellow splodge marks the route.

13 On the road, turn right, and then left at the T-junction, past a stream-side cottage, to run up to a double railway arch. Follow under and up the steep hill for 100m and turn left at the top. Still climbing, the memory of the lush valley bottom a distant memory, run past a grand house on the right and driveway on the left. At the end of the garden of the house on the right, turn into what looks like a driveway, but soon turns into a bridleway going straight up between hedgerows.

14 After a while of climbing, Higher Knowle Wood appears on the left, but ignore any path, until you hit the road at the top, and a fingerpost sign and gate on the left show you the correct way north. The path is now flat and the going good. After a gate, the descent steepens until you hit a road at the bottom. Keep on to a crossroads and then turn left. Take the next right, signposted 'dead end', and right again to pick up a winding lane, through cottages with thatched roofs. Mr Baggins must live here. This is the southern entrance to the village of Lustleigh.

15 Pass to the left of the cricket pitch and under the old railway arch, shared with a stream, along the same path, which turns sharp right and then left to come out at the memorial and church. Primrose tearoom is situated on the left, opposite the Celtic Cross, and a good place for a brief stop. For something more medicinal, The Cleave pub is off to the right here, but bear in mind, there is still some way to go.

16 Carry straight on, with the church on the right, to the crossroads and on towards a childrens play park, inside what is known as the Orchard, past the public loos and a car garage. Here, atop a granite boulder is a throne, used as a spot to crown the May Queen. Inscribed are the names of the Queens over the years.

The Hobbit Half Marathon

Highland cow on Dartmoor – MB

17 At the far end, the path continues, through a gate and up a steep, stony path. Bear right at the junction and up to another gate by a field with a huge rock in it. Cross the field to another gate and turn left after going through the gate.

18 Another gate gives access to a good, flat path, marshalled on each side by wrought iron gates at intervals, and a stable on the left. A path joins in from the right at a gate, where a tarmac drive, by a house and outbuildings on the left appears. Follow the sign and fingerpost towards Hammerslake and turn left to go past the house and over a small bridge. The path winds its way through woodland, climbing steadily until it eventually meets a gate, and comes out on to a road.

19 Turn left here, and after a short while, turn right up a path by a house called The Grove. Ignore the faint path off to the left, but instead climb up through large, rocky outcrops and huge boulders on an obvious path. The trees eventually give way to the summit of Sharpitor, and the path bears right, frustratingly still climbing.

20 The path handrails the wall on the right and gradually opens on to the summit of the hill, littered with gorse bushes, as it bears left. Hunters Tor comes into view, so head towards it as it meets a wall. Pause to take in the view of the valley below.

21 Cross the wall, either at the tor or the gate, and follow the path down and to the right. The path meets a hedge and turns sharp left, through the edge of a field, through a gate and into a farm. Head straight ahead, to reach a T-junction between path and road. Turn left to follow a good path down to Foxworthy, a small hamlet of refurbished farmhouses.

The Hobbit Half Marathon

22 The path passes in front of the large, thatched house and heads down towards the bridge. However, before reaching the bridge, turn left in front of the other houses on a waymarked footpath to enter woodland through a gate. About 100m after the gate, a signpost marks a junction, so turn right here and head down to the river.

23 Upon reaching the river, head downstream and left to a crossing point provided by large boulders. The river passes underneath and through the boulders beneath your feet, so take care, as these can be slippery in the wet. On reaching the other side, the path turns left, downstream, before climbing uphill and right. Keep left at a junction to climb up the steep valley side to reach a house on the left and a gate.

24 Go through and turn immediately left in front of the house, before turning right at a fingerpost after only a 100m, signed for Manaton. One more uphill on a steep but wide track, flanked by high earth works.

25 On reaching the top, go through the gate and turn left on to the road which leads you back to the car park.

South East

With a higher population density than much of the moor, the lower lying south-east of the moor is spattered with hamlets and villages serving the farming population. In recent years many of these settlements have become commuter hot spots, the arterial A38 running along the national park's south-east boundary providing the perfect link up and down the peninsula.

For us off-road runners that means more fields and stiles to negotiate, alongside rivers and historic byways and fewer tors. However, don't expect it all to be golf course-style, manicured footpaths. Ryder's Hill in this area is the south moors highest summit and is not only quite remote, but also typically boggy.

Leusden Common (Route 24) – SW

Venford Brook (Route 25) – SW

21 Antique Commuters Break – Ashburton

Winter trail - MB

Distance	8km (5 miles)
Ascent	215m (704ft)
Grade	T1a
Start / Finish	Village centre car park SX 755 699 (50.5157 -3.7572)

Known as the gateway to southern Dartmoor, Ashburton is a busy little town. Its proximity to the main Devon Expressway, or A38, may have something to do with its popularity, but it is also home to a good selection of inns and plethora of antique shops. There is good parking in the centre of town, and a public loo. For light lunches there are numerous cafés and a deli, so even though this run is a short one, you might find you spend slightly longer exploring the town.

This route is on good trails and waymarked footpaths. There is also a section or two on road, but these are rural lanes with very little traffic. There is a working farm to pass through, and while the route follows a public footpath through the middle, please respect the owners and stick to the path.

Due to the nature of this route, you could get away with road running shoes in the drier seasons, although the valley bottom can get muddy after rain.

This route is ideal if you are in the area or driving between Exeter and Plymouth and fancy a leg stretch. It is ideal too if the weather is grim up on the moor, but you don't fancy running around the roads.

Note: the car parks do charge for their use so come prepared.

21 Antique Commuters Break – Ashburton

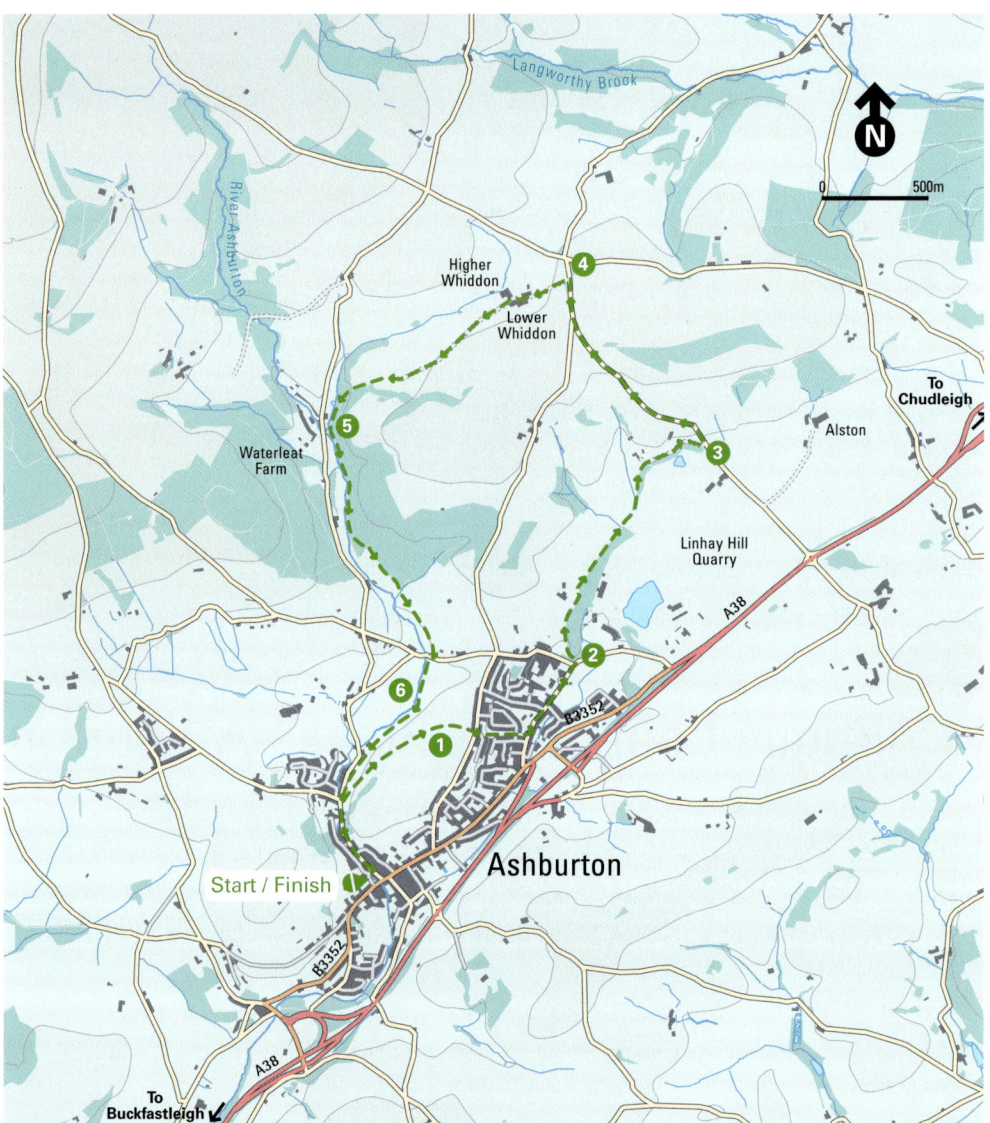

Route

Head north out of town before turning east past the local college along the national park boundary. Head north again to reach farmland above the village. Turn left at a farm to face west, and then south to follow a river valley alongside woodland and pasture land back into town.

Detailed directions

START From the car park in the centre of town, run downhill until you get to the high street via the small bridge. Turn left and run past the play park on the left. Keep going ahead to the Victoria Inn also on

Antique Commuters Break – Ashburton

the left. Just before a left turning, turn right up some steps marked 'Terrace Walk'. After the gate, at the fork, take the right footpath uphill past a few benches. Continue to the gate by the woodland at the end.

Perfect trail. - MB

1 Go through the gate and follow the path down through the trees to a road at the bottom. Go straight over and slightly left to pick up another path which descends to another road in an estate. Turn left and follow to a school on the left.

2 Go past the school and, at the junction, go straight on and after only a few metres turn left and back on yourself at a footpath sign. Follow as it bends round along a fence line to the right, climbing slowly. The path becomes wider as it contours an old quarry on the right and continues to climb.

3 At the top of the path, the surface changes to tarmac and you stay right at the fork. Keep climbing, and after another house on the left, again stay right at the next fork. At a T-junction, turn left and carry on steeply uphill along a rural road.

4 Eventually, at the top, a road goes off to the left, but keep going straight on before coming to a crossroads. Turn left down a road to a farm, where the path makes its way through the farm, and left once out on the other side. The track now climbs up gently, before descending all the way down to a river.

5 Do not cross the bridge and instead, turn left to follow a muddy path through the edge of a woodland. Ignoring the paths off to the left, follow the river valley to the right before crossing a road after a stile. Go straight ahead into the field and follow the obvious path, handrailing the trees on the right.

6 Eventually the path starts to climb, up to the left of a barn and re-joins the path at the entrance to the field from before. Cross over the stile and go down the steps to the road. Turn left and follow the road back into town.

Dartmoor cross – ML

High on the south moor – SW

22 North from Ivybridge

Distance	12.2km (7.6 miles)
Ascent	352m (1,155ft)
Grade	T2a
Start / Finish	Harford Road car park SX 636 562 (50.3907 -3.9197)

Now quite an affluent commuter town for workers travelling east up to Exeter, or west to Plymouth, Ivybridge is the southern gateway to Dartmoor. It is also the start, or finish, of the Two Moors Way, which links Dartmoor to Exmoor.

Apart from Dartmoor itself, Ivybridge's skyline is dominated by the large chimney from the now redundant Stowford Paper Mill first established in 1787. The premises are in the middle of being renovated into houses and a shopping arcade, but the chimney is set to remain.

The town is large and has everything needed as a base from which to run; from inns and cafés to shops and supermarkets. There is also ample parking in town, at one of the many pay and display sites.

The centre point of this run is the River Erme, and the route goes high up one side, crosses over, and comes back down the other. The climb from the start on to the moor is cheeky and long, but starts on lanes and is not technical in any way.

Route-finding is relatively easy, and you only need your wits about you once on the top ridge. If in doubt, or in bad weather, just return the way you came and attempt the run on another day. The moors are not going anywhere in a hurry.

22 North from Ivybridge

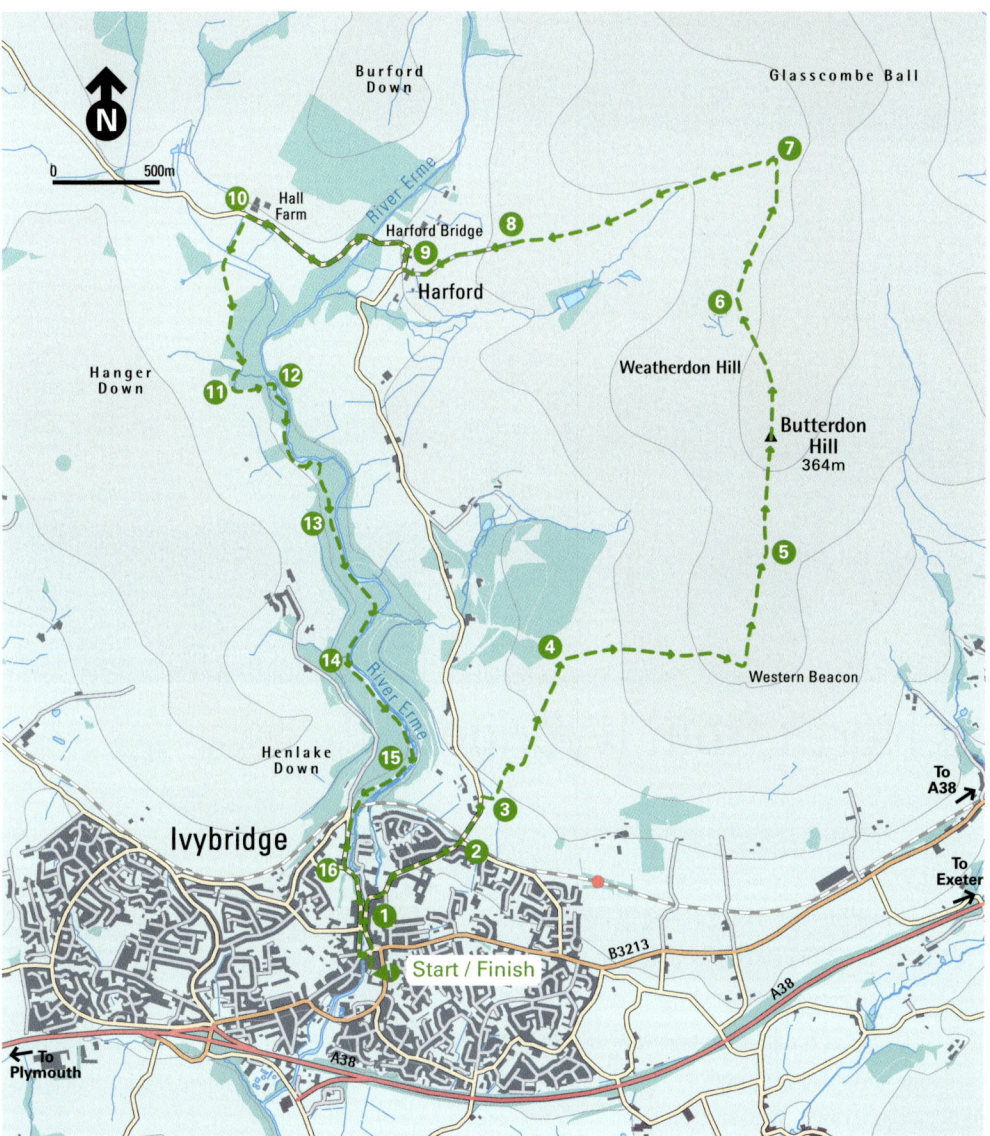

Loos and facilities can be found adjacent to the main car park, and the run does not enter any military training areas.

Route

Head north out of town past the college and on to the moor via the waymarked Two Moors Way. Climb up to Western Beacon, then north over Butterdon Hill, before turning west to pass through the hamlet of Harford. Once over the river, turn south via riverside footpaths and trails back to Ivybridge.

North from Ivybridge 22

Western Beacon – SW

Detailed directions

Standing stone – SW

🏃 **START** From any of the car parks in town, head for the town centre and tourist information point where you will find the start of the Two Moors Way. My preferred car park is situated just below the old mill, conspicuous by its tall chimney.

① Either follow signs for the Two Moors Way, or Ivybridge Community College, to go up a road on the right-hand side of the river, climbing gently at first. As the road climbs more steeply, it leaves the river behind and makes its way first past the college, and then to a crossroads. The road has a pavement, so is safe to run on, although the gradient may have different ideas.

② At the crossroads, head straight on to cross over the main South Western Railway line and southern boundary of the national park, still following the signs for the Two Moors Way. The lane no longer has a pavement but the gradient is easier, and only 200m of the road remains before you turn right at a sign and farm, to gain a track heading up on to the moor.

Old mining settlements – SW

③ The wide track swings immediately left and continues to climb. The track is easy to follow being flanked on both sides by low trees and hedgerows. Keep climbing to a gate, which opens the run out on to the southern moor. A faint track carries straight on, but instead turn right to head for the summit.

④ The grass path is easy to follow, and after a short while crosses a wide, stony track. Keep on uphill as the path becomes narrower and steepens on its approach to the summit of Western Beacon. Take in the

North from Ivybridge

views and a much-needed breath before turning left and north to follow a good, downhill trod along a line of boundary stones.

5 Descend to a small, muddy pool, often dry and aptly called Black Pool, and carry on straight ahead to start another climb (much shorter this time). Pick your way along the boundary stones and path to the top of Butterdon Hill, marked by a concrete trig point and numerous cairns.

6 The plateau across the top is flat and easily runnable, but a good trod over to the left is the best line which gradually descends to an obvious boulder known as Hangershell Rock. Continue to the right of this rock to gain the main Two Moors Way, here a wide track, turn right on it and follow it for a short while.

7 At a boundary stone and obvious stone row and earth works, turn left and slightly downhill. The track is narrow but offers good running as it contours around the valley with a small plantation over to the left. A small stream runs into this valley making the low ground very boggy, so stay on this track as it climbs gently and then descends again. For the adventurous amongst you, feel free to descend directly from Hangershell Rock, but do not expect dry feet or fast running.

8 As the path bears right, away from the plantation on your left, look for a boundary wall which comes into view, and converges on a small car park. Pass over the cattle grid to access the road, and follow this downhill to the hamlet of Harford.

9 On passing the church on the right, turn right and follow the road around in front of the church and then immediately swing left, downhill to Harford Bridge. The traffic here is generally light but be alert all the same.

10 Ignoring the path on the left just before the bridge, cross over and continue along the road, left and slightly uphill. After just over half a kilometre, a farm on the right appears and directly opposite is a signed footpath. Pass through the gate on this footpath and follow to a makeshift bridge over a stream.

11 The path now crosses a field diagonally left to a gate in the corner and then handrails a small woodland on the left. At a stile and gate, cross into the trees and descend on a woodland path. At the far edge of the wood turn left, and do not take the path straight ahead and right. Instead, follow a wall to descend to the banks of the River Erme through a gate.

12 Turn right and follow the river, through woodland. The path generally stays close to the riverbank, and many paths lead right, up away from the main track. Ignore these and stay straight ahead on the waymarked footpath.

13 The ground is runnable, but littered with tree roots, and is boggy in places as streams flow down from the slope above. The path has been maintained with wooden duckboards, but tread carefully.

14 After a while, the path becomes wider and much firmer. Picnic areas are now ubiquitous, but the plethora of bins show this area is well-maintained. There will probably be more people encountered now as you close in on the town.

15 After passing a weir, placed to power the Stowford Paper Mill, the railway viaduct comes into view, and the most interesting of routes is to bear left and under one of its huge arches on a good path. This follows the riverbank closely and brings you out on to a road by the entrance to the mill.

16 Turn left and follow the road back to town, its sustenance, and car parks.

Dartmoor's Snowdon

Choose your path

23 Dartmoor's Snowdon

Distance	12.8km (8 miles)
Ascent	418m (1,583ft)
Grade	Grade F2
Start / Finish	Holne Church SX 706 694 (50.5108 -3.8261)

At only 495 metres or so high, this Snowdon on Dartmoor is nothing like its namesake in Wales. Its shape, relative unpopularity, and the fact that there is no train station or café on the top are also other factors when realising this summit bears no resemblance at all to its Welsh counterpart.

Snowdon Hill is in fact the second highest summit on the southern moor, and this run does visit the highest; Ryder's Hill (515m). Snowdon itself was a significant place for the Bronze Age folk with numerous cairns dotted around, as there are too on the slightly lower summit of Pupers Hill.

The tops of this trio of summits are far more accessible for those who wish to climb them, and while the views may not be as mountainous, they are still extremely worthwhile compared to the relative effort made in running to the tops.

However, what is guaranteed is that you are far more likely to get lost trying to find the top in poor weather than the highest peak in Wales. The featureless nature of this part of the moor, makes route-finding challenging in mist, so bear that in mind before deciding on this particular run.

The run involves a considerable amount of climbing for the distance, but even so, does not venture past any tors. It sounds like I am not really selling this to you, I know, but if remoteness and good, moorland

23 Dartmoor's Snowdon

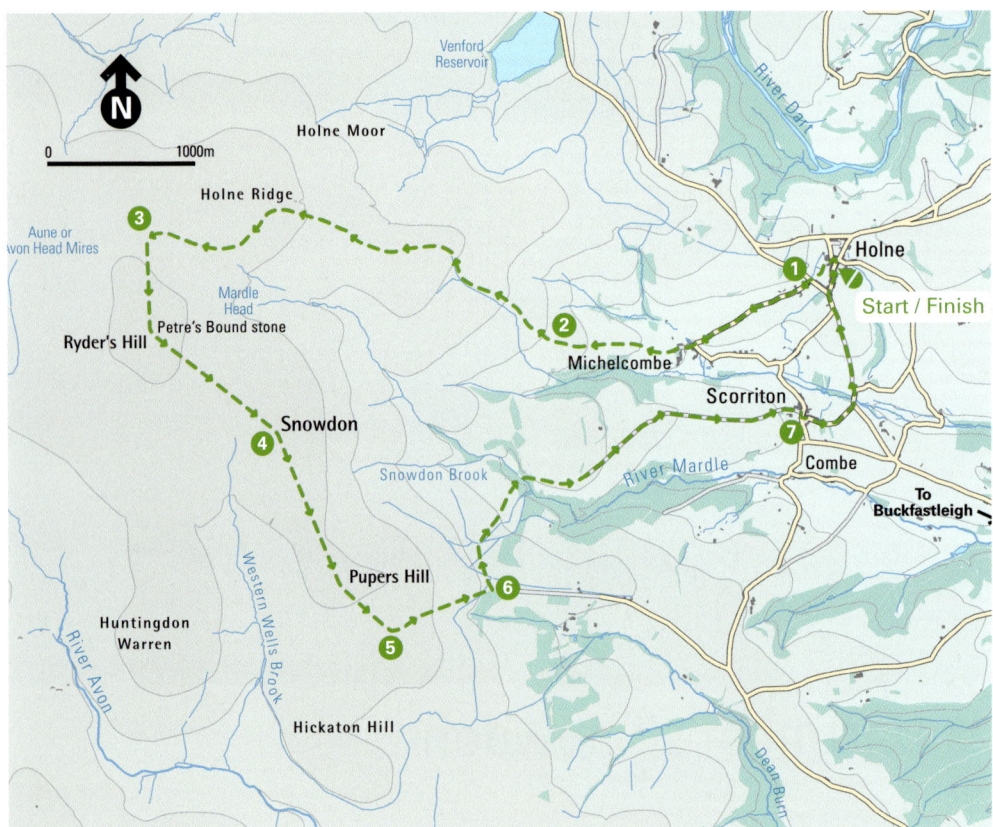

running, coupled with a great pub at the start and finish is your bag, then this route is for you.

I tend to choose this route because it guarantees a workout and good preparation for fell races further north. It is not the driest of places and is moist for most of the year, making it excellent training.

The route starts in the splendid village of Holne which hosts a great community run shop and café, and a very welcoming pub called the Church House Inn, situated next door to the church, obviously. Parking is available on the road between the pub and café in a small car park, although it's often busy at the usual times, so park with discretion.

As mentioned above, check the weather and your ability to map read before running this route if you are not familiar with the area. Ryder's Hill was once a checkpoint for the Royal Marines, '30 miler', commando test, but was later deemed too remote in case of needing a casualty extraction from the summit, other than by helicopter. At this point I should note, with puffed out chest, that Ryder's Hill was still included on the route when I went through training.

Trail shoes, in the drier months, will be fine here, particularly as there is a portion of road at the start and finish, but I would wear studded fell shoes in the wetter seasons on this run.

Dartmoor's Snowdon 23

The south eastern moor above Holne

Route

From the church, head south-west to Michelcombe, then west up on to Holne ridge via a rough path. At the top of the ridge, turn left to climb up to the trig point of Ryder's Hill, Follow the ridge south over Snowdon and Pupers Hill, before turning east to cross a steam and return to Holne via the hamlet of Scorriton.

Detailed directions

START From the main entrance steps to the church, go through the gate and up to the church front, then turn left to follow the waymarked path alongside the gravestones and into another field with more recent headstones. Go diagonally across to a gate, then through another pasture field to a gate which leads on to a narrow path before meeting a road.

❶ Go slightly right and straight over at the junction to follow a road downhill, signposted to Michelcombe. At the bottom, cross a bridge, pass through the small hamlet and carry straight on up the hill on a wide track. Ignore the path off to the right and keep on uphill to meet a gate which opens on to open moorland.

❷ Ignoring the obvious vehicle track off to the left, carry straight on to the tree ahead, where a faint track continues up the hillside. Lots of trods, man-made and

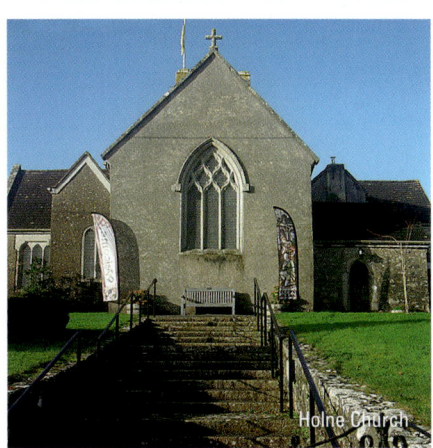
Holne Church

The edge of Snowdon, not the Welsh one!

Looking up to Pupers Hill

Dartmoor's Snowdon

livestock-made, cross the main path but stay straight on in a westerly direction, continuing the climb up on to Holne Moor, and towards Holne Ridge. Eventually, the path tops out at a crossroads by a boundary stone. **Note**, if at any part you are going downhill, you have gone too far, or have gone the wrong way.

❸ At the ridge, turn left and head south to climb the last bit to the summit of Ryder's Hill, helpfully marked by a trig point. There is a track which leads directly to the summit, but this can turn a little mushy in the winter.

❹ Carry straight on and slightly left towards the next summit, which is Snowdon. A faint trod marks the way. Not many other routes ascend this top so this should be fairly obvious. A cairn marks the way, before a slight incline leads to the top.

❺ Following in the same direction, stay on the flat ridge's apex, initially downhill then up to the standing stones of Pupers Hill. From the summit, carry straight on in the same direction for a short descent before picking up a crossroads, where you need to turn left. A wide track leads downhill towards some trees and, for the purpose of route-finding, stay on this definite path towards Lud Gate.

❻ On approaching the boundary, turn left before the gate, to follow the boundary on a good path until meeting a river and footbridge. Cross this and climb up to a gate and go through. The track becomes more definite and wide, before descending on the Two Moors Way in to the hamlet of Scorriton.

❼ At the road, turn right, then first left and continue to lose height to a T-junction. Turn left and just after crossing the bridge over the river, at the sharp right-hand bend in the road, continue straight on up a steep, stony bridleway. Ignoring all other paths, continue on to a road and carry straight on. At the first right, turn and follow back into the village and some welcome sustenance.

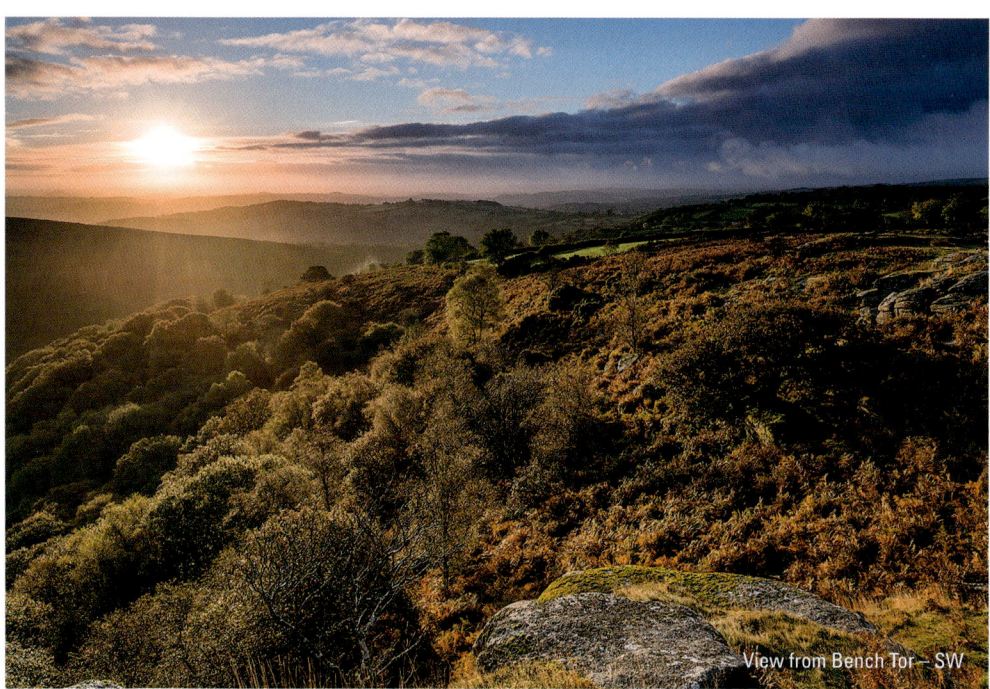
View from Bench Tor – SW

24 Tour of the Dart

Distance	20.9km (13 miles)
Ascent	746.7m (2450ft)
Grade	T3b
Start / Finish	Venford Dam car park SX 685 712 (50.5262 -3.8555)

The River Dart is probably the most recognisable river on the moor, and even gives its name to the national park. The West and East Dart rivers meet to form one waterway that eventually flows out to sea at Dartmouth. It's a popular destination with kayakers, and when the water is high enough, they can be seen parked at either end of what they know as 'the loop' starting from New Bridge (visited on this run) and ending at Holne Bridge.

This run is a wonderful meander over the south and north banks, passing lots of spots for refreshments along the way, season dependent though. Despite the distance and climb, it is generally a recovery run for myself, the ground being very runnable.

On occasion, I have shortened this route to avoid a stretch of road, and enjoy the stepping stones at Dartmeet, but all too frequently these are overflowing and impassable, and the inevitable detour is somewhat disheartening. To that end, this route goes the long way round to avoid disappointment, although I have included some reference to it in the detailed description.

On the way round, there are numerous ice cream vans, an inn, a café, a loo at the start, and two more on route. The opening hours and presence are relative to the season and weather, although it is not unusual

24 Tour of the Dart

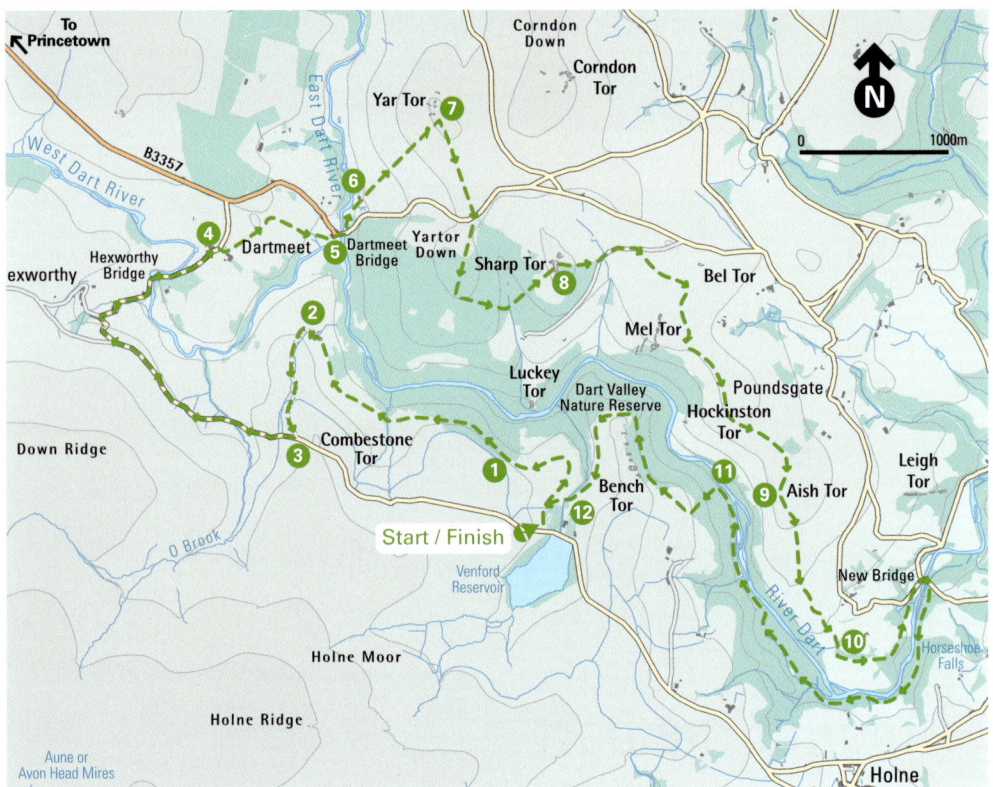

to find a hardy ice cream van perched at the top of Bel Tor Corner in all weathers. What can I say? The Devonians love a Mr Whippy!

The route is generally sheltered, and trail shoes are fine on this run, as there is nothing too technical about the ground. However, the route is fairly committing in that once you cross the river early on, there is no crossing point until much further along the route, and by then it is quicker to carry on to the finish than to retrace your steps.

Finally for the romantics among us, part of this route, high on the north side of the Dart, goes along Dr Blackall's Drive. This was built by Thomas Blackall in the 1800s to ride his carriage along, and enjoy the views while in residence at Spitchwick Manor in the valley below. One legend tells that his ghost can still be seen travelling along this track, such was his love of this part of Dartmoor. Another tale tells the story of his wife who, becoming too ill to ride on the moor on horseback, had this carriage track made so that she could still ride out and enjoy the view. Whatever the truth, why let it get in the way of a good story! It is indeed a great track to run on and enjoy the views it provides.

Park at the northern car park, across the dam by the loos.

Route

Head north on a path that quickly bends west to follow the southern hillside of the River Dart. Turn left, uphill, at the farm to a road and turn right. Follow the road to a bridge via an inn and head north-east on

Tour of the Dart 24

Dartmeet stepping stones – SW

paths to Badgers Holt and cross the River Dart. Head north east up Yar Tor, then south to take in Sharp Tor before turning east to descend to New Bridge. Cross back over the Dart and turn right to follow the river bank and hillside back to the reservoir.

Detailed directions

START From the car park, head directly away from the road and out of the back of the car park, with the woodland on the right. There is a faint path that crosses over a small stream and heads out towards the Dart valley ahead. This path then becomes more obvious and bends left to contour the valley side, high up above the river.

1 The rugged path now enters some woodland. This is a popular spot for Dartmoor ponies, and can get a little rough under foot, so watch your step. On exiting the woods, the path bears left again to cross a stream via a small clapper bridge or ford, as is your choice. Follow this path gently uphill now to meet a gate and go through to follow a bridleway to a farm at Combestone.

2 Go through the next gate and turn left to follow the , uphill to another gate and cattle grid.

Note: At this point, there is a short cut which is made by turning right after passing the farm to follow

135

Tour of the Dart

the path down to the river and across the stepping stones, as mentioned in the initial route description. However, only attempt this in the summer and after periods of little rainfall, or you could be disappointed. Don't be tempted to cross if the stepping stones are not visible unless you want a one way, wet and wild ride to the coast.

❸ If going the long way round, continue up the farm track, through another gate and up to the road. Turn right. For those who are anti-tarmac like myself and believe roads are for cars, feel free to run on the left-hand verge, handrailing the road until reaching the bridge and cattle grid at the bottom. Cross over and climb the road to a junction, and bear right down a steep hill, which hairpins past the Forest Inn, and then down to Hexworthy Bridge. Cross over, noting the good swimming spot on the left, and climb the road up to a chapel on the right. Some 200m past this, turn right, following the footpath signs, and then immediately left, before entering the farm ahead.

❹ Pass through the gate and follow the waymarked path up, across the field. The way is marked by small, wooden, ground signs. The path descends, then turns right through a gate to descend steeply down a stony bridleway. Take care here as this is rough going. At the bottom, turn left to enter a field and run carefree on great ground down to a building, to the left of which is a gate where the footpath goes.

Note: for those that took the shortcut, this is where crossing the stepping stones would have brought you out and you can re-join the main route.

❺ Go through the small gate by the side of the building and follow to the road at the top. Turn right and cross the bridge with care, as traffic often misjudge the bend and the steepness of the road. Once across, turn immediately left and pass through the car park, heading to the far end. There are toilets, and in the right seasons, refreshments to be had here. There are also the remains of an old clapper bridge, now replaced by the new road bridge.

❻ At the end of the car park, there is an entrance to Badgers Holt, a café and shop, and just before its entry on the right is a small gate with a footpath sign. Take this and follow until it opens out on the right. At this point, turn right on open moorland to climb to the top of Yar Tor. There are trods which lead to the top, but as long as you keep going up, you will reach the summit, rocky tor sooner or later.

❼ At the top, turn right to follow a path to the road and cross into a small car park. Here there are two paths, but take the right one, leading up to the top of Yartor Down. It's a short climb, but well worth it for the view of the River Dart below. From the top, turn left to look across a small valley to another rocky tor, complete with a precariously perched tree on the top. Find the small trod, and keeping left descend to the bottom and then up again, on an obvious path to the summit of Sharp Tor and its tree.

❽ A track leads down from the top to a road, turn left here to follow the road to a wall corner. Turn right to follow the wall to a gap between two walls where an obvious track goes through. On the left, in a small car park, there is often an ice cream van for those in need.

❾ Follow the wide track, known as Dr Blackall's Drive as it contours around the valley. The route bends right at a wall corner to go around Aish Tor on the left, and as the path turns left, a small thin track appears on the right, descending down a spur. This track is a must, so turn right here for a wonderful, whooping, downhill adventure. The track is narrow but good and bends right then left, before bending

Tour of the Dart 24

Guardians of the crossing – SW

right again to the corner of some trees inside a wall. This is called Deadman's Corner. If in doubt as to the direction on this decent, keep heading down until you get to the river.

10 At the bottom, turn left along a good track, to follow the river down to a car park, again with an ice cream van and loos. This is a popular spot with tourists and kayakers so expect it to be busy. At the road, turn right to cross the bridge, again taking care because of traffic. Once across, turn right again to find a gate with a waymarked signpost. Take this path and follow the bank of the river. A major path, marked Two Moors Way climbs off to the left, but ignore this and stay on to the right. The path climbs up and away from the river for a while, through thick woodland, and then descends again to end at Sharrah Pool, a favourite swimming spot. Just back from this is a steep, uphill path that follows the line of a wall and this is your route.

11 Turn left up this steep track, which hugs the boundary to its left. It is steep and on difficult ground but soon emerges out of the trees and on to a wide track to the right. A gate on the left confirms your position, so turn right to follow the path which contours above the treeline and high above the river. The track re-enters the woodland, and sweeps left with the valley side. Follow the track until a stream appears on the right, which is the outlet stream from Venford Reservoir. Turn right to cross through the ford here and left once on the other side. The flow is regulated here, so the stream can be always crossed. Those who don't want wet feet can carry straight on to cross the dam at the top of the path.

12 Once over the river, climb the steep bank on the path handrailing the wall on the left and at the top, turn left to return to the car park.

Dr Blackall's Drive – SW

River Avon

25 South Brent Bimble

Distance	22.5km (14 miles)
Ascent	550m (1,804ft)
Grade	T3b
Start / Finish	Old railway station car park SX 698 602 (50.4277 -3.8342)

Described on the Visit Dartmoor website as *"South Devon's best kept secret"*, South Brent is indeed a fine village although as for being a secret, I would probably challenge this description. No village of South Brent's size would have such a wide range of amenities without high numbers of people to partake of such. Furthermore, as a base for a long run up the Avon valley and the surrounding moorland, this should not be overlooked. In just a couple of streets, you will find a pub, cafés, a deli, a butcher, chemist, a fish and chip shop, the ubiquitous charity shop, florist, DIY and garden centre, arts and crafts shops, hairdressers, bank (rare in towns nowadays, never mind villages), a community centre, post office and even a computer and IT store.

It even had its own train station, which up until 1964, was on the main South West line. The train station now forms part of the local industrial estate and the main building is now a dentist. This is also the site of the local, free car park, designed for visitors, but with the increase of folk working from home, this is now used almost exclusively by residents during the day as well as the evening. If no parking is available here, there is nearly always some along the road by the village hall, on the opposite side of the track to the station.

25 South Brent Bimble

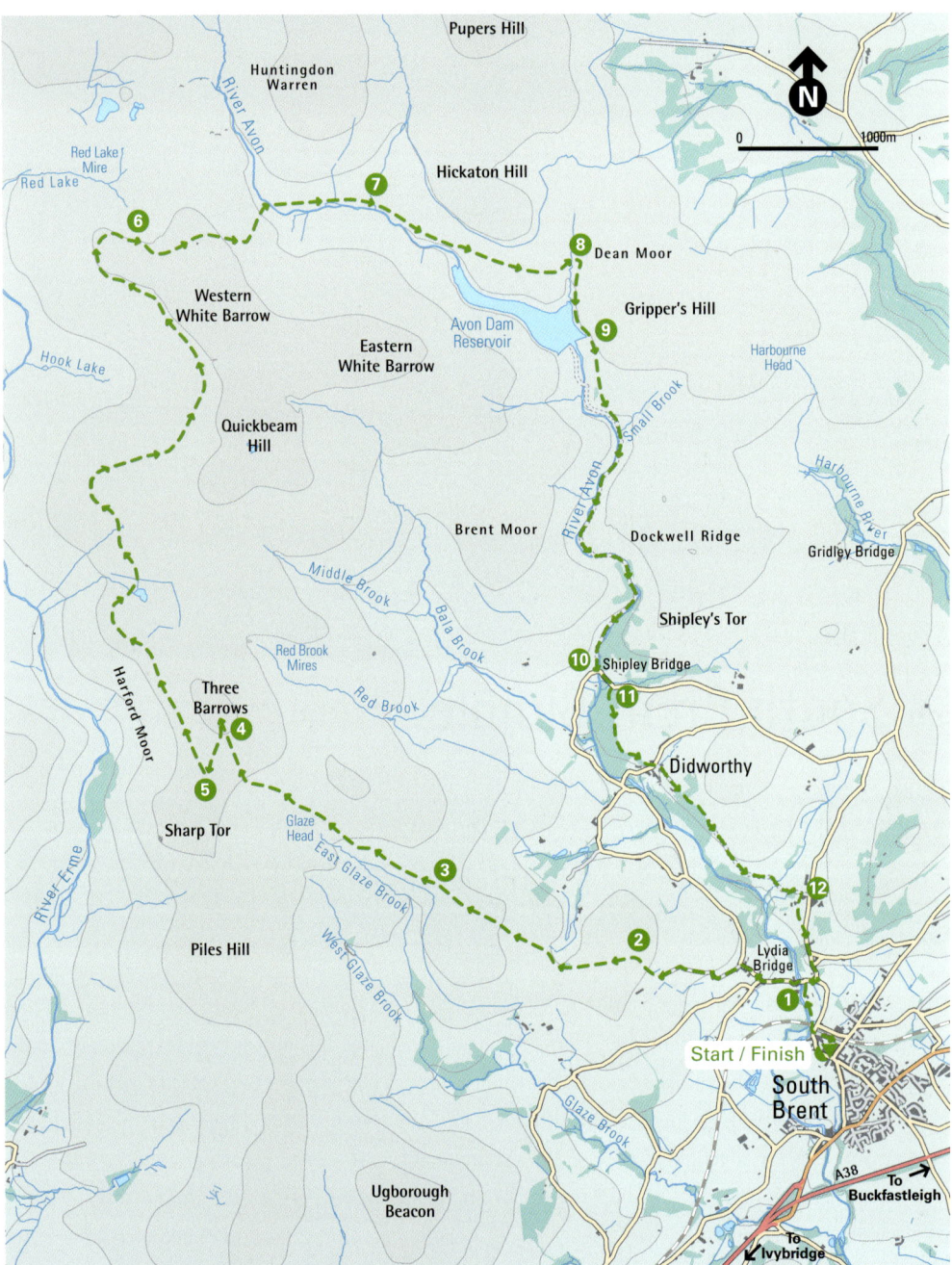

With very little through traffic, South Brent retains its charm and is somewhere to spend a little time after a long run. Situated on the banks of the River Avon, the village was originally a woollen market centre boasting two annual fairs, and although these have long since gone, the village still retains this market feel.

The route itself takes in some the most outstanding scenery and features, west and north of the start. Fourteen miles is a long run but included here is a shorter option, although this shortcut does miss out

South Brent Bimble 25

Pigs at Shipley Bridge

some of these features. Also be forewarned that as South Brent is low-lying, the first part of the route is all uphill, albeit at a gentle enough gradient.

The run climbs up to Ball Gate on lanes and bridleways before reaching the open moorland. Ball Gate is a very ornate double gate, seemingly out of place, but is a remnant of the grounds of South Brent Manor.

The next part of the run is on open moorland but does follow a grassy trod, so navigation is not too challenging. Once at the top of the hill, the route follows the Two Moors Way on what is locally known as the Puffing Billy Track. The old railway from the 'Volcano', where a former mine was established deep in the heart of the moor, is easy to follow and solid underfoot, it is also popular with cyclists.

The route then descends to the River Avon and over a great example of a Dartmoor clapper bridge, before then following the river back via moorland paths, a reservoir, lanes, and public footpaths.

However, it is worth a slight dog-leg out and back, off the main route, to an old mining chapel at the grid reference SX 666 666. The chapel is now just a depression in the ground, with a low wall around it, but the steps to the low alter and a granite block with a cross inscribed on it, remains. The chapel is not marked on the map, and is often confused with a small ruin, fifty metres to the south. Finding it can be a challenge, but head up the line of the stream to the ruin and go past it, to a small, rocky outcrop. The chapel is below that.

The chapel came into being in 1909 thanks to Keble Martin and his brothers who used to have a camping holiday up there every year. Sons of the Rev. Martin, they built it initially to shelter out of the weather. A cross was inscribed, and a morning service was held there. (*Over the Hills*, autobiography of Keble Martin, 1968).

As for the grid reference, isn't this the sign of the devil? Food for thought ... ?

The longer of the two routes does climb up on to exposed moorland so make sure you check the weather and dress accordingly. If your navigation skills are not up to scratch, the moor can look very inhospitable. My advice would be to get to the point on the route where the shorter option breaks off and make the call then. At the Shipley Bridge junction, there is a public loo, and an ice cream van during the popular seasons.

25 South Brent Bimble

Route

Head north out of the village following the river, before turning left uphill to head to Ball Gate initially via road, then a track. The shorter option now turns right to follow the boundary wall down to Shipley Bridge and re-join the main route.

The longer route carries on north west to the main Two Moors Way track. Turn right and head north for a while, turning east before Red Lake to descend to the River Avon. Turn right to follow the river past the reservoir and follow the footpath from Shipley Bridge back to South Brent on the east side of the valley

Detailed directions

START From the old railway station, now a Dental Practice, and the car park, turn right and run up the road to a T-junction. Turn left and then immediately right down a footpath by the side of a house, following the footpath sign. The route goes under the railway line and then along the side of the River Avon. Go through a gate and on to some steps, which lead on to a road by a bridge.

❶ Turn left over the bridge crossing over the river and follow the road uphill as it swings right. This is the start of the long climb. Ignore the road on the left and carry straight on past some houses to a T-junction, with a red phone box on the left. The phone box now houses a defibrillator, perfect after that first climb! Turn left here and follow the lane up to a farm. The road now turns 90 degrees right and becomes a bridleway. Follow to a gate.

❷ Once through the gate, turn left to follow a faint track across a field. The track becomes more prominent as it descends and turns into a bridleway. Go through another gate and climb gently all the way to the very large and seemingly out of place Ball Gate. For the longer route, now go to point 4 to continue. For the shorter route, read on.

❸ Short option – At this point, the shorter option of route turns right after the gate, to follow the edge of the moor along a wall boundary. The path then becomes more definite as it descends to a road. At the road turn left and follow to Shipley Bridge. Re-join the route now from point 11.

❹ Main route – Once through the gate, carry straight on to find a faint, grass trod. You are aiming to the left of the hill in the foreground. The route follows the line of East Glaze Brook over on the left, and the trod becomes more definite after a short while. The brook's source is soon easily identified by the marsh over to the left, but carry straight on, still climbing, as another large hill ahead and slightly right comes into view. This is Three Barrows and our summit goal for the day.

Keep to the trod, aiming slightly left of the hill to meet an obvious, low, boundary wall, characterised by small rocks covered in heather and moss.

Turn right to follow the boundary, still climbing, to reach the summit, covered with piles of stones.

❺ From the trig point, in this case a concrete pillar, turn left, almost back on yourself, to follow the obvious track down and right to join the main Two Moors Way track. The views in good weather over to the Erme valley are immense.

South Brent Bimble 25

Avon Dam Reservoir

6 At the main track, an old mine railway, turn right and climb gently. This is easily runnable but can flood after heavy rain. The track bends right, over a bridge, then left as it contours efficiently around the hillside, leaving a small, pit lake behind. Another swing right and then left takes you under Quickbeam Hill, and eventually to a right-hand hairpin bend with views over to the small, volcano-shaped spoil heap on the left. The Red Lake spoil heap and the water feature below also known as Red Lake are the remains of the old china clay works. However, this route does not go to the end of the line, and instead turns right at an obvious Two Moors Way marker stone, just off to the right of the main track.

7 Turn right here to follow an obvious path up and round a small hill. Ignore the old tramway on the right, and instead bear left on the grassy path to descend steeply downhill towards the River Avon below. A faint trod leads down to a classic, Dartmoor clapper bridge, which you must cross to continue the route. Turn right after the bridge and pick up the uneven path following the line of the river downstream.

8 The path here is often wet, and is very uneven, and the footfall, river and climate take its toll, so watch your step. Eventually a small wall is crossed, and Huntingdon Cross is just on the other side. A small tributary comes in from the left, and time, weather and energy allowing, (it is nearly all downhill now to the finish) it's worth a quick visit to Keble's Chapel. Follow the right-hand side of the stream heading for the ruin. This is not the chapel. Once past the ruin, head to a small cluster of rocks, and just below this, between the rocks and the stream is the low depression of the chapel, marked with a small, crossed stone at one end. Retrace your steps back to the cross by the stream / river junction after your homage.

9 The path continues to follow the river downstream, and eventually a view of the Avon Dam Reservoir comes into view. The path skirts the left-hand side of the upper slopes of the body of water, and swings left to descend to a ford over a stream. After crossing the ford, turn right and follow the banks of the reservoir, heading for the left-hand side of the dam. The brightly coloured life rings help in poor visibility.

10 A stone track continues, down the left-hand side of the valley, away from the dam, and again follows the line of the river. The track soon becomes a tarmac road, and makes for easy running down the valley,

25 South Brent Bimble

River Avon above a clapper bridge

giving you a chance to recover and enjoy the view. The road is a service road for the water authority, so rarely has traffic on it. It crosses the river via a bridge and now follows the other bank. Notice the potential bathing spots and waterfalls on the left now.

11 Ignoring the road off to the right, keep following the river to a T-junction. A car park and loo are situated on the right here and it often hosts an ice cream van, so make sure you carry some cash.

12 Turn left here to cross the cattle grid, and immediately take the waymarked footpath over a stile on the right, entering some woodland. The path is easy to follow now, and numerous public footpath signs mark the way. Keep left and then eventually come out on a road. Go straight over, up a track past houses, and once through a gate, enter woodland again.

13 The path is now more a bridleway and descends to a ford before climbing, for the last time, up a gentle slope to a small hamlet. At the road junction, turn right to follow the road downhill to another T-junction. Turn right here to head for the bridge over the River Avon, visited near the start. Turn left just before the bridge on to the footpath that you started on, to head back to the village of South Brent.

Central

This area comprises the central part of Dartmoor, around Two Bridges and Princetown. To the north and south are gradual transitions to high Dartmoor hills and tors, whilst in other directions there are changes from open moorland to enclosed fields and farmland. Plantations here are not uncommon, with the outer, high relief protecting the trees from the brunt of the harsh weather systems, common place in the west.

Eylesbarrow Track (Route 26) – SW

Babeny stepping stones (Route 29) – SW

Princetown Dash 26

Heading from Peatcot to Princetown – SW

26 Princetown Dash

Distance	7.2km (4.5 miles)
Ascent	141m (461ft)
Grade	T1b
Start / Finish	Princetown visitor centre SX 590 734 (50.5441 -3.9909)

As Princetown is such a central location, it makes sense to have more than one run from the settlement. This route is so-called as it shares the name of the race that once took place from the Plume of Feathers Inn. The inn has one of the many bunkhouses in the area, and what could be better than falling out of bed, and into a pub for breakfast? Unfortunately, due to the recent pandemic, this has been forced to close and at the time of writing the brewery is trying to find a tenant. However, there are other places to eat, drink and stay within the village.

The route is short enough, along with only a relatively small amount of climbing, to be justifiably called a 'dash', and as such, makes a fantastic early morning leg stretch with no real navigation required. Run, turn left, turn left, turn left and your back where you started. It can be wet and boggy in the middle section, but exposure along the route is minimal for Dartmoor. I would wear trail shoes all year-round on this, due to most of the route being on good tracks.

A key point of interest on this short, fast route is somewhat sobering, and that is the plaque at the start of Conchies Road, about two thirds of the way through the route. The wide track that approaches the farm upon which you run, travels someway into the middle of the moor, and then just ends for no apparent

26 Princetown Dash

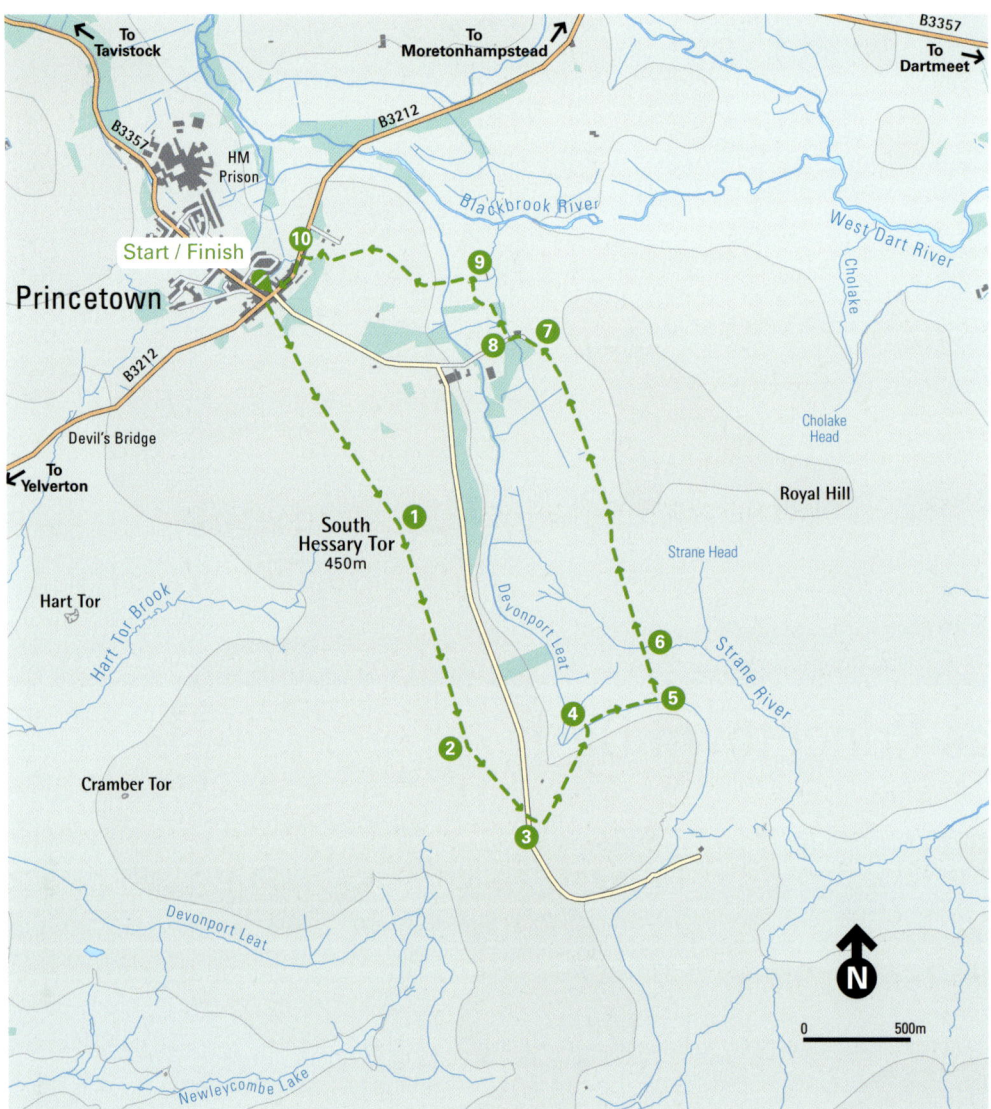

reason. Conchies Road, as this track is known, is so named as it was built by a group of men during the First World War who were conscientious objectors.

Those that defied the 1916 Military Service Act, meaning compulsory military conscription to the army for men aged 18 – 41, on moral or religious beliefs were 'employed' elsewhere, and in 1917, Dartmoor Prison was used to house such men. While never actually called prisoners, they were housed at the prison and paid a wage. Employment took the form of shaping stones, and building 'the road to nowhere' now known as Conchies Road. The land was to be reclaimed for the purpose of agriculture, but Dartmoor has never been for turning, and this proved a fruitless (excuse the pun) task.

While not prisoners, with no locks and keys, few guards and no uniform, conditions were vile. They worked in the bleak Dartmoor weather, food was basic, the prison conditions were grim, and the local population disowned them as cowards. Many did not return home; some because they died, and others because

Princetown Dash 26

Bullpark – SW

their own local community shunned, and in some cases, abused them for not standing up to fight.

Route

Head south out of town and then, at the end of the boundary wall, turn left to cross a road and run down a farm track to Peat Cot Farm. Follow the leat, then turn left to follow another boundary on the left on moorland tracks. Turn left again on footpaths past the next farm, back into town.

South Hessary Tor – SW

Detailed directions

START At the roundabout in the middle of town, face the Plume of Feathers Inn, and head down the lane to its left, which finishes at a gate, and turns into a wide track on the other side. Go through the gate and climb gently to another gate at the top.

Heading to Peat Cot – SW

❶ The track now opens out on to more exposed moorland, but the track is good and the block of South Hessary Tor comes into view. Follow the track with a stone wall on the left, all the way to the tor, which is the highest point on this run.

❷ Descend now, still on the same track, until the wall on the left ends and turns ninety degrees left. Follow the stone wall now over moorland to meet a road after approximately 340 metres. At the road, turn right and then left at a sign for Peat Cot. Note, there is a diagonal track from the wall corner to the entrance drive by the sign to Peat Cot, but it's not well-defined and can be wet and boggy for little or no extra gain. Your choice.

149

26 Princetown Dash

A Dartmoor resident – SW

❸ This is a farm vehicle track and it descends left along a good surface to a gate, and eventually on to Peat Cot Farm. Look out for the noisy Border collie, secure in the field on the left, which seems to have been there for many years.

❹ At the gate to the farm on the left is the old Wesley chapel, now a bothy-type accommodation, which offers a fire and a dry roof. After the gate, head to a fingerpost sign over a leat, and turn right to follow the leat on the left-hand bank. This is the well-known Devonport Leat and is always flowing.

❺ At the wall / leat junction, use the stile to cross the wall, and turn left to descend from the bank of the leat. Follow the path, downslope now, using the wall on the left as a guide. The path follows the direction of the wall for some time, wending its way in relation to the ground conditions.

❻ A small footbridge makes the first stream crossable, but as the slope climbs gently again, the ground can be wet and somewhat boggy. Keeping dry feet is a challenge all year-round and impossible in the winter. Pretty soon the track becomes broader and more definite, following the line of the wall, and is flat, providing good running.

❼ Eventually, with a farm in front, a track meets your path from the right. This is the Conchies Road. Head through the gate in front of Bullpark Farm and look for the plaque on the gatepost.

❽ Follow the concrete road left, downhill, and then right at the bottom to head along a wide track with a stream on the left. Go through the gate and follow the track as it rises up and left, to another gate. The track then flattens again and runs on to a fingerpost, with a track junction.

❾ Turn left up the hill to a gate and cross the leat at the gate. Continue uphill to the top on the obvious track, which swings right and then left to go around a plantation. The path then descends after another gate, past a house with another noisy collie. At the final gate by the house, go careful, as the path finishes on a main road.

❿ Turn left along the pavement and back to the start.

Wistman's 'Spooky' Wood   27

Wistman's Wood – SW

27 Wistman's 'Spooky' Wood

Distance	7.2km (4.5 miles)
Ascent	127m (418ft)
Grade	F1
Start / Finish	Two Bridges Hotel SX 609 750 (50.5586 -3.9648)

For those not accustomed to running on uneven ground and indistinct paths this is a great introduction to fell running as the route follows broken paths and moorland, but only for a short section. The rest of the route is on good tracks which are easy to follow. There is, however, the upper section of the West Dart river to cross at a weir, so this route should only be attempted after and during periods of dry weather or, at the most, light rainfall. Even then, you will get wet feet.

The route heads out to Wistman's Wood, one of three remaining ancient English oak woodlands on Dartmoor, the last vestiges of the primeval forest that would have covered much of Dartmoor in pre-historic times.

The wood is an English Nature Reserve and a SSSI, and is best known for its trees, stunted in growth as a result of the harsh winds, and the copious amounts of lichens and mosses, rarely found in such variety elsewhere in Britain. However, perhaps the location owes its popularity to the legend that the Dewer, Devonian for the Devil, chooses this wood as the resting place for his demon hounds, or wisht hounds. My kids always thought this wood was haunted, due partly to the fact that we would always leave it till dusk to visit, so as not to encounter many 'grockles' (tourists).

27 Wistman's 'Spooky' Wood

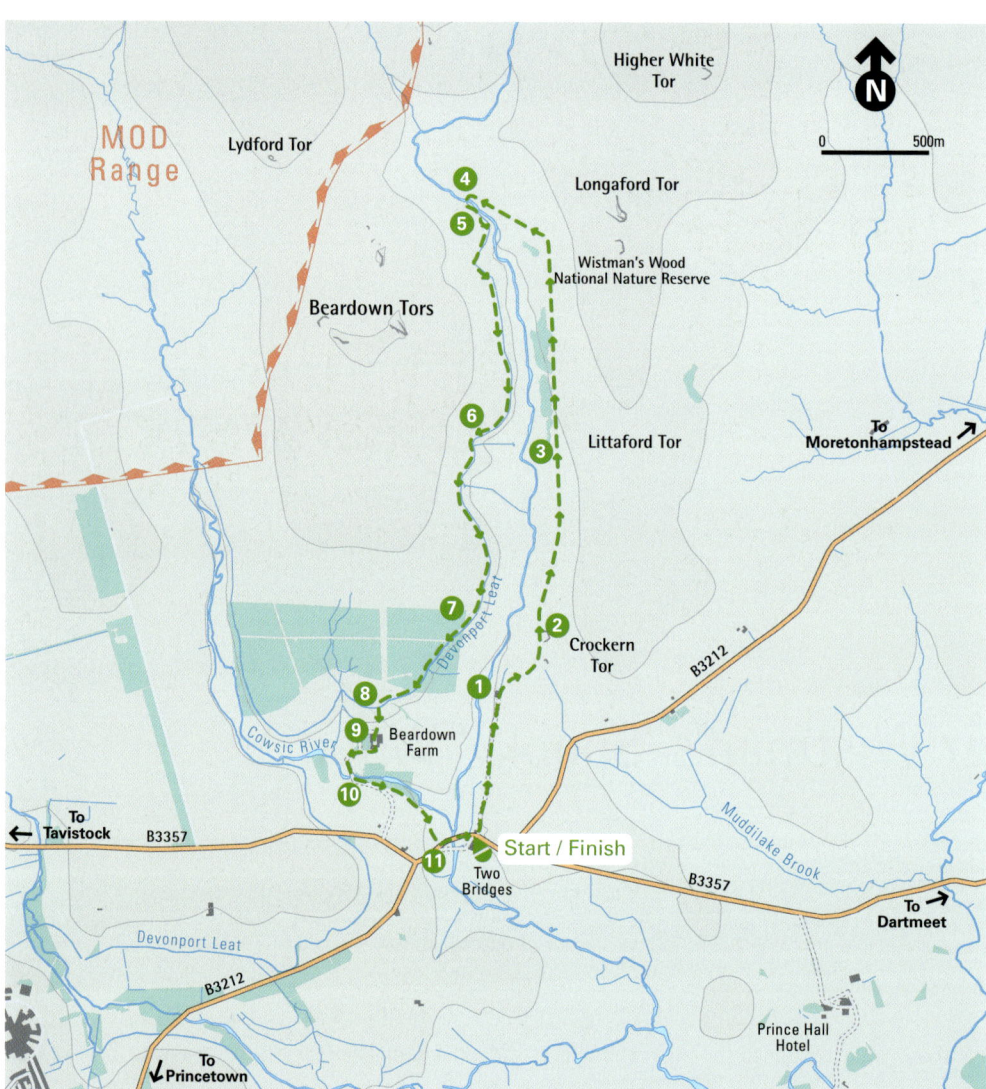

The route returns, after crossing the West Dart river, along the origins of the Devonport Leat and back to the start via another much younger forest, and a working farm, via footpath signs and stiles a plenty. The car park at the start, while convenient, is small and often full at peak times but a concession can be paid at the Two Bridges Hotel opposite to park your vehicle. Just pop into reception and pass over some coin, £5 for four hours which is cleverly refundable against the purchase of food or drinks. I recommend the cream tea here, although the ubiquitous Dartmoor Jail Ale is equally temping.

Route

Head north up the track to the woodland and pass it, keeping the woodland on the left, Cross the river on the left by the weir, and turning left follow the leat to a farm before following waymarked paths back to the start.

152

Wistman's 'Spooky' Wood 27

Wistman's Wood – SW

Detailed directions

START Leaving the car park, hotel and road behind you, pass through a wooden five bar gate, and with the stone wall on the left, continue on the hard track to Crockern Cottage.

1 The path skirts to the right of the cottage and starts to climb along more rough but obvious tracks. After a 100m or so the gorse clears and the path splits. Take the left fork across a muddy stream, using the granite stones and boards, towards a break in the stone wall ahead.

2 Continue on this well-trodden path, watching your step, or testing your dexterity on the rocks and divots as you like. This type of terrain, while fun, can be a test of one's foot placement and unless experienced, can unbalance the unwary. Don't expect to set any speed records here.

3 Over to the left is the West Dart river and ahead is another stone wall and stile. Climb or vault over and Wistman's Wood appears ahead. The main track veers to the right and starts to climb though larger boulders. Keeping the wood to the left follow the now faint track, most tourists having stopped at the woods to return from where they came. Route choice is up to the individual, but keep heading in the same general direction. On passing another stand of woodland, start to look for a track that heads left, down towards a wall and stile next to the river. Longaford Tor should be over to your right at this point, a conical shaped pile of rocks, and is visited on another run, but use it as a navigational feature all the same.

4 Upon reaching a wall turn right and follow to the stile. Over the stile you will be able to see a man-made weir and hut where the Devonport Leat originates. If you have overshot it, you will know as the river

Wistman's 'Spooky' Wood

bends sharply to the right and there is nowhere to cross. The water here is usually shallow as you cross the weir, but take care as the water flows quickly, and the stones can be green and slippery. At this point, if the river is flooded and looks unpassable, it probably is, so instead save it for another day and retrace your steps back to the car and pub.

5 Climb the stone steps and then turn left to follow the leat which flows off to the right of the river. It is better, and more runnable, to stay to the left of the leat and a clear, if thin, path is easily moved along.

6 The leat now flows for a good while as it contours the hillside. Follow this, staying to the right of it, taking care at the numerous flood gates situated at regular intervals along the way. Good vistas of Wistman's Wood over to the left, across the other side of the river, are a distraction when running at speed, so watch your step.

7 As the leat meanders, the next feature you are aiming for, a coniferous wood, appears briefly, and then disappears. After one last clamber over a makeshift bridge over the leat, enter the wood and continue along the line of the waterway.

8 On exiting the wood, the leat continues on, under a wide track bridge. Turn left here to face a farm with a clear sign pointing towards it.

9 The path is directed right just before entering the farm itself. Follow this direction through another gate, and trot easily along a wide gravel track, which turns left then sharp right, always descending gradually. This is the farm's main driveway so take care and look out for tractors.

10 The track, after a hundred metres or so, crosses the Cowsic River, over a concrete bridge. At this point, turn immediately left off the main track to find a path over tree roots and boulders, which follows this minor river downstream.

11 This path, although well-trodden, is an assault course of green rocks, peat and fallen trees, not to mention several stiles. However, the fun only lasts for half a kilometre, and in no time at all, you meet the main road, whereupon you turn left and back to the start. This road, while seemingly minor, is the main thoroughfare across the moor, so stay alert and tucked in for the final 150 metres.

Gunpowder, Treason and Plot   28

Higher White Tor, looking east

28 Gunpowder, Treason and Plot

Distance	10.9km (6.8 miles)
Ascent	311m (1,019 ft)
Grade	F2
Start / Finish	Postbridge visitors car park SX 646 788 (50.5935 -3.9135)

Postbridge – a honeypot for visitors from all over the world if they come to Dartmoor just for the day. Famed for its ancient 13th Century clapper bridge, many come to photograph and cross it. There are many clapper bridges on the moor, but this is the easiest to access with less than 100m walk from the car park. Situated almost slap, bang in the middle of the national park, it's an obvious place to start a run. The visitor centre has all the information to hand about the area and wider park, and has toilets to boot. The car park has a tariff of £1 for three hours, which is enough for this run. If it is full, or you are lacking a pound, you could always try parking across the road for free in the Bellever Forest car park just over the cattle grid, but this fills up quickly, so get there early. Other places to park close by are limited and frowned upon by the national park.

The post office opposite the bridge has a small shop for cans of pop, bottled water and confectionary. Sandwiches and pasties too, if you are lucky.

As this particular run is quite short, and if the weather is good, the green field by the bridge is a great spot to leave the rest of the family to play, paddle under the bridge and have a picnic. Bellever Forest also has some short walks to complete, and the East Dart Hotel has a beer garden and offers pub meals.

28 Gunpowder, Treason and Plot

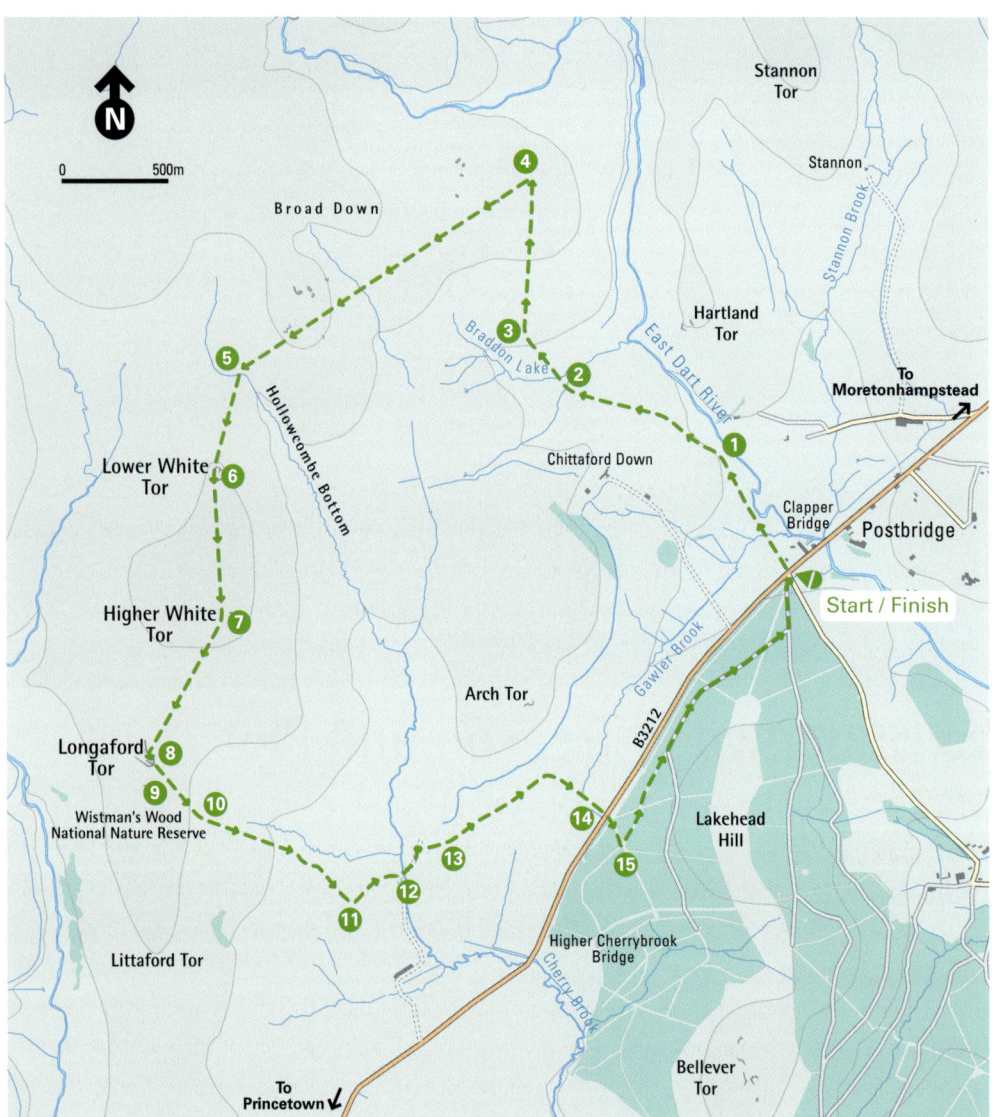

Close by, and on the route of the run, is the Powdermills gunpowder factory, long since closed for production after the invention of dynamite. Dating back to Victorian days, the settlement had some eighteen buildings, with quarters, offices, stables and even a school. This was needed as often over a hundred folk were employed at any one time at the factory. The gunpowder, or black powder, was made for the quarrying industry locally and a few of the buildings remain to explore, including the chimney. The remoteness of the factory is not an accident, nor is its closeness to a good water source, namely Cherry Brook. A license to place a public house here when the factory was in full swing was refused, on the lines that alcohol and gunpowder in the same hands didn't mix!

The buildings close by now house a small pottery and craft centre.

The route of the run is easy to follow in all weathers, and although exposed on the high ground, is sufficiently runnable to keep warm and moving. The ground is generally good and varies from good, wide

Gunpowder, Treason and Plot 28

tracks to open moorland. Some of this moorland can be wet, in-line with the rest of Dartmoor, but not enough to sink into and prevent a good stride. There is quite a bit of ascent but this is at the start on fresh legs.

Whenever I run this route, it is rare that I see anyone, after leaving the car park, and not again until entering the forest. It is remote enough to discourage those drawn to the bridge and wary of the moor. For that reason it is a route I use a lot in all weathers, when perhaps the military ranges are busy to the north and west. Upon reaching Longaford Tor, I often claim that this is my favourite run on Dartmoor. Until the next run in another location that is.

Route

From the main Dartmoor National Park car park in the village, head north-west on the west bank of the East Dart river and climb via a well-used path to Broad Down. Turn left, following a wall to reach a stream crossing before heading due south to cross Lower White Tor, Higher White Tor, and eventually Longaford Tor. Then turn left to descend east to a chimney and then on to cross the main road into Bellever Woods, before turning left again along forest tracks and back to the village.

Detailed directions

START From the main car park adjacent to the visitor centre, a path leads around to the left of the building to gain the main path. Turn right and head away from the road and downhill. Ignore the less popular path off to the left and carry straight on. The path is narrow but well used, and so is in generally good condition for the first part. The farmland drains from the left to the river on the right and you will cross several drainage ditches via single, granite, stone blocks.

1 As the path flattens out, it becomes briefly soft underfoot, until it then climbs along a fence line and another solid path to reach a gate. Pass through this and follow the stony, granite-strewn track along the line of a wall on the right of you, still climbing gently away from the river valley. Views over to the right of the East Dart river and Hartland Tor now appear.

2 The path now becomes less defined, as the many ramblers choose their own line across the ground which is flatter and often soft. Whichever line of path you take, keep the wall close to the right. The path descends to a confluence of two small streams which can be crossed without getting wet feet at the junction, if care and a degree of dexterity are used.

3 Once across, climb steeply up the bank ahead for a short, sharp shock to cross a dry leat and be faced by a wall with a stile in front of you. Ignore this stile, and instead follow the wall left to a corner where two walls meet. The footpath now turns right, through a gate, and the ridge of Broad Down looms up ahead. Numerous paths now climb steadily, but for ease of navigation and guaranteed good ground, follow the line of the wall, keeping it to your right.

The gradient uphill is uniform and runnable if you like a good workout. As you work up a sweat, eventually a wall from left to right comes into view on the ridge ahead. Although there are lots of stiles to cross along

Gunpowder, Treason and Plot

the length of this wall, I prefer the security in poor weather of handrailing the wall to your right until it meets the adjacent wall in the corner.

❹ A metal gate, to the left of the corner, opens easily and once through, turn left to follow the wall on your left. The higher lumps of Broad Down are up to the right and worth the extra effort if confident of keeping the wall in view, as a fingerpost of your direction.

Follow the line of the wall, either alongside it, which offers a good well-trodden path, or parallel to it on the higher ground. Run along a rollercoaster of peaks and troughs, crossing a stream and the remains of old tin workings, to climb to the rocky outcrop overlooking a steep descent to a wall corner and deep stream. The running is quick here and not arduous under foot until you meet the stream.

❺ Turning half left, cross the stream using the large rocks and keeping your feet dry, climb away from the wall, as it instead follows the valley downhill, to a large boulder up the slope. Lower White Tor lies ahead now, uphill on a clear, moorland trod, up an easy gradient. The route crosses a quartz vein, some of which pokes through the moorland grass when short.

❻ Crossing through the rocks of Lower White Tor, its higher sibling by 20m now lies ahead to the south, and although the uphill gradient is easy, it is a double-edged sword. The ground being flatter is often also wetter, and a dry line to Higher White Tor is hard to come by. Still, it's a welcome cooling of the feet on a summers day and it lasts but a short while before the ground hardens, and a tall, wooden stile gives you access across the wall.

❼ Higher White Tor is the highest point on this run and is just the other side of the wall once crossed. Either passing through it, or around to its right, you will see a wide, well-trodden path swooping down to Longaford Tor below, which stands like a big, tower block. A granite stone early on in the line of the path leans towards the tor, as if pointing you in the right direction.

The gentle descent offers good running, with the odd exposed bit of peat to leap, but nothing too taxing to breaks one's stride. Head straight on to the tor.

❽ When stood at its northern face, late on a summer evening, with the sun low, Longaford Tor blocks out the light as it towers above you. It's too tempting not to ascend to its summit, and this is best done from its southerly side. The views here are worth a short pause; over to the west is Wistman's Wood on the banks of the West Dart River and start of the Devonport Leat. To the south there are views over to Princetown and Two Bridges, but it is to the east that we are interested in on this route, the chimney stack of Powdermills below the treeline of Bellever Woods, and Tor of the same name.

Descend down to the smaller crag to the south, below the main tor, and pick up a thin trod descending to its left, heading to a T-junction where two walls meet, and are directly in-line with the chimney. However, stop short of meeting the wall, instead following the trod bearing right, contouring a few metres above the wall. Look for a break in the wall, and cross between two gate posts on an obvious path.

❾ Now turn to face downhill and due east, following the line of a small stream. Stay to the right as another path heads directly left and down the slope, offering a quicker line. Trust my local knowledge here and stay right, still descending and heading for the buildings of Powdermills. The ground is marshy as it flattens out but if the advice is heeded, there should be little issue.

Gunpowder, Treason and Plot 28

Longaford Tor, before the gloom

10 The path now swings left towards the chimney as you approach the treeline so follow it heading over to a gate in a wall, marked 'LICHWAY'. Descend the path, passing the chimney to its right and descend the fence line to a wooden signpost and track.

11 Turn left here on the wide track and cross Cherry Brook via a bridge. The track heads uphill past the factory buildings on the left for 100m, before you make a right turn at a faded sign and along another wide track to a gate.

12 The track sort of peters out here at the low, marshy ground (sheep and ponies turn over the softer ground) but head slightly left, almost parallel to the woodland and road over to the right. The track improves as you stay left and slightly higher, and then suddenly becomes more obvious as it turns sharply right across the marsh. The path is well-maintained here and easy ground takes you to a gate which leads directly on to a road, so take care here, particularly if dogs are in tow.

13 Cross the road directly, with good visibility either way, to another gate which leads into the Forestry Commission managed Bellever Woods. The path is easy here and flat, and brings you, after a very short while, to a crossroads and a wooden signpost.

14 Turn left here, signposted towards the *'Visitor Centre 1.6km'*. The broad track offers a quick finish and easy running in contrast to the softer ground crossed earlier. Turn left downhill at a T-junction to a gate which opens up into a forestry car park. Pass through this on to a road and turn left to cross a cattle grid. The visitor centre is just across the main road ahead, where you began.

Sharp Tor in winter (near Route 29) – SW

29 Long Circuit South from Postbridge

Yar Tor summit – SW

Distance	19.8km (12.4 miles)
Ascent	530m (1,738ft)
Grade	T3a
Start / Finish	Postbridge visitors car park SX 646 788 (50.5935 -3.9135)

Postbridge is a honeypot for visitors, as are a couple of other locations on this Dartmoor run. Bellever Tor and Dartmeet, both taken in on the route are both popular with tourists as they are easily accessible without much effort. The enjoyment of this run is that it links up these spots via relatively quiet footpaths, and the effort required to go between them makes one feel mightily sanctimonious. Those people slurping ice creams, having just fallen out of their cars and made the 50 yards across the car park, will not even notice you, so fixated are they on their sugar fix.

The route is different to many on the moor and typical of this area. It seems more friendly and safer than the high, north moor and follows definite footpaths and tracks for the most part. However, the distance and amount of ascent involved do make this a serious run, so be prepared.

Loos and facilities can be found at the start and at roughly the halfway point, although these are seasonal so don't rely on them after hours or out of season.

The route is best started from the national park car park next to the visitor centre and toilet.

29 Long Circuit South from Postbridge

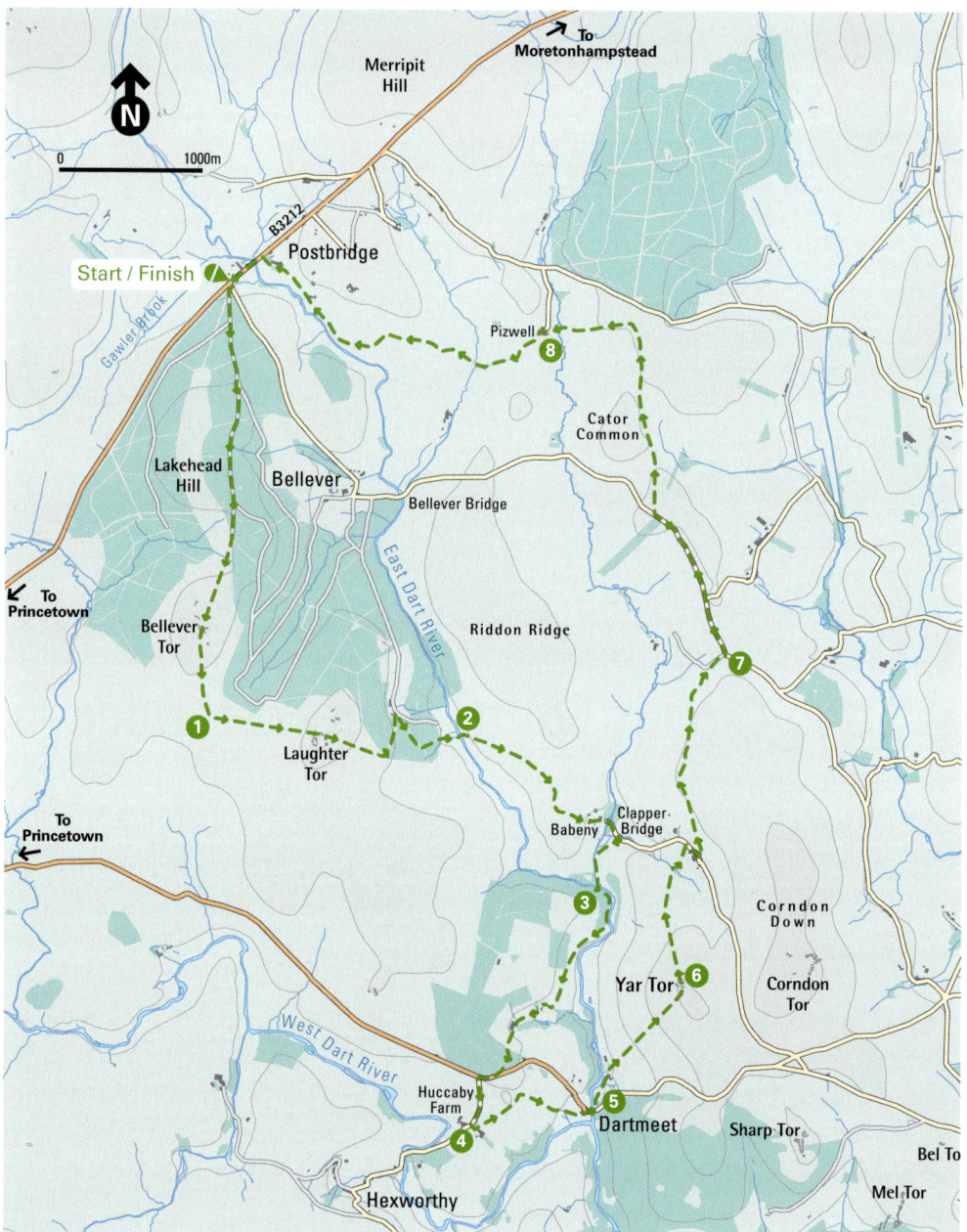

Route

A long, circular route which starts by heading south to Bellever Tor and Laughter Tor, before following the East Dart River to meet its counterpart; the West Dart River at Dartmeet. The route now crosses the river in an easterly direction before heading north-east up to Yar Tor, and then north through farmland to the southern edge of Soussons Wood. Finally, the run turns west to follow footpaths back through Pizwell farm and on, back to Postbridge.

Long Circuit South from Postbridge 29

Bellever Tor at dawn – SW

Detailed directions

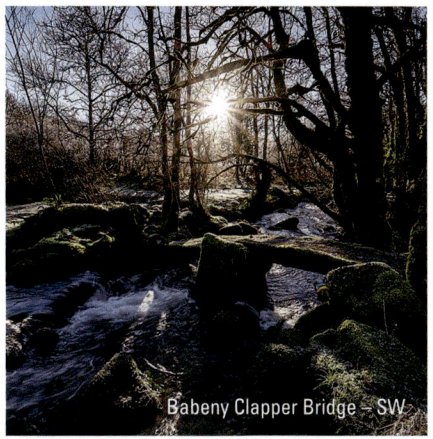
Babeny Clapper Bridge – SW

START Start by running to the left of the visitor centre from the car park to find a footpath. Turn left and follow for a short while to the road. Cross over and go straight ahead across the cattle grid, and then turn right into the Bellever Forest car park. Go through the large metal gate and run up the large, wide forest track straight ahead. This is waymarked and eventually, after a long, gentle climb, comes out on to the moor at the bottom of Bellever Tor. Climb up to the top via the track.

1 Go straight over and follow the track down the other side to a gate in the corner of a wall. Go through and turn left to follow a track up to the summit of Laughter Tor. At the top, turn right and follow the track down to a wall and, after going through, turn left and follow to a gate in the wall which leads into a plantation. Go down the track, and choosing the right fork, descend to a house and look out for a path on the right, going back on itself. Turn right here and follow this narrow path as it turns sharp left and heads down to the East Dart River.

2 At the river, cross via the stepping stones, and turn immediately right up the obvious path. This leads eventually to a gate and then down to a farm where the track is marked through a farm. Follow this through the yard and on to the farm drive. Cross the bridge and climb gently up. After the stream crossing turn right on

Bellever Woods – SW

163

29 Long Circuit South from Postbridge

a footpath by a bench, and keeping right aim for the stream. Cross the small footbridge on the right to the other side of the steam and turn left following the waterway downstream to meet the East Dart River.

③ Use the stepping stones to cross and then turn left on to a rough path along the river's edge. The path heads up to the right, away from the river, and goes through a series of gates before meeting a farm. Signposts guide you through the farm and, keeping straight on, follow the wide, vehicle track to a crossroads. Go straight until you meet the road. Taking care on this busy road, turn right and then after only a short distance turn left, down a minor road.

④ Look out on the left for a footpath to a farm before the chapel, and turn left here, then left again to go through a signposted gateway. Go across the fields and at the end turn sharp right down a steep, rocky path. At the bottom turn left and cross the field to a gate by a house. Go past the house and out on to the road. Turn right and cross the bridge at a place called Dartmeet.

⑤ Once over the bridge, turn immediately left into the car park. A loo and refreshments are, at times, available here. Go to the end of the car park and find the footpath through a gate, to the right of a place called Badgers Holt. Once out of the trees, at the first opportunity turn right and climb the steep hill to the top. There are many paths, but just keep heading up the best line to the summit of Yar Tor.

⑥ At the lofty summit, turn left and descend the clear path along the ridge-line to a stile and gate in a wall. Go through and follow the path along the wall line, down to a bridge over a stream. Go straight over and, obeying the route markers, go to the left of the farm and out on to a lane. Turn right, and once past the farm on the right, turn sharp left up a footpath signed 'track' and up on to open moorland. Follow this track through ancient field systems, until it meets a road by a small passing place.

⑦ Turn left here to run along a flat road for a while. Ignoring the turning on the right, keep straight on to a strip plantation on the left and right. On the right, a footpath sign directs you through a gate, go through and follow the path on the other side which handrails the boundary on the right. The path soon becomes more obvious and meets a path crossroads. If you reach a road, you have gone too far. Turn left at the crossroads here along a fence line and down to cross more stepping stones over a brook and up into an old, medieval farm.

⑧ Go through the farm and turn left at the option to follow a track, which turns right and descends down to a stream, where unfortunately at this point they forgot the stepping stones. Cross the stream and follow the track uphill. After a while the path fades as it crosses fields, but at a wall corner, turn left and follow the path down and then right to cross through gates and, once again, on to a better track. This becomes even more definite as it approaches a house on the right, and eventually turns into a road. Follow this all the way back to Postbridge, turning left at the main road, to cross the bridge and back to the start.

Winter clouds, Hart Tor (Route 9) – SW

Autumn evening clouds over Black Tor (Route 10) – SW

Longer Excursions

Dartmoor has much to explore and, time allowing, long runs can easily be facilitated with a bit of imagination or by following one of the National Trails which pass through the Dartmoor National Park. These include the Dartmoor Way, West Devon Way, Two Moors Way and the Abbot's Way, all of which have their own guides and literature available.

Listed here are just two of my favourite longer routes which can be achieved in a day, although the Dartmoor Crossing lends itself to a less stressful, two day adventure with the option of a pint, or two, in Princetown.

As these routes involve up to a full day out, I would suggest a minimum kit requirement of the following:

- A litre and half of water in a bladder or three, 500ml soft flasks or similar.
- A waterproof jacket with hood, and waterproof trousers.
- A spare, long sleeve top.
- Running tights, if not already worn.
- Hat or multi-functional headwear and gloves.
- Emergency bivvy bag.
- Personal first aid kit.
- Food and snacks for the trip (personally I wouldn't rely on just gels and / or getting a feed at any of the stops, just in case they are closed).
- Route description (from this book), and map and compass.
- Headtorch if doing the route in the short, winter days.

Poor excuse for a path (Route 31)

Crossing the East Okement River – AF

30 Dartmoor – Top to Bottom

Distance	56km (35 miles)
Ascent	977m (3,206ft)
Grade	T3a
Start	Belstone village green SX 619 935 (50.7247 -3.9566)
Finish	South Brent village centre SX 698 602 (50.4277 -3.8342)

There is something very satisfying about running the length of Dartmoor and in the fast-growing world of ultra-marathons, this is indeed an ultra, albeit a baby one.

There are many discussions as what constitutes the optimum route, where to start and finish, and in which direction to do it. However, for the purpose of this book, I believe this route to be the most functional while also taking in perhaps the most attractive and easily runnable terrain. Admittedly this is a balancing act, as although this is not the shortest and most direct route and does not follow the more traditional route of the Two Moors Way (a Devon coast to coast route through Dartmoor and on to Exmoor, and the coasts at each end), it has numerous villages strategically placed along the route to act as refuelling stops or as an option to bail out if tired and / or injured.

I have chosen to describe this route from north to south, mainly as it feels like running downhill, and because technically, it is exactly that. The beginning at Belstone starts at higher altitude than South Brent at the finish. Running from end to end does involve a degree of planning and forethought, let alone a good deal of

Dartmoor – Top to Bottom

running. So, either drop a car at the finish, so enabling a drive back with a friend to pick up the car from the start, or get a friend or loved one to drop you off and pick you up.

Public transport in Devon, while excellent between the main towns and cities, may involve a few more connections to get to the respective start and finish.

The route itself breaks up neatly into manageable sections:
Belstone to Postbridge – 18.08km (11.3 miles) – 492m ascent (1,614ft)
Postbridge to Hexworthy – 7.20km (4.5 miles) – 145m ascent (475ft)
Hexworthy to Princetown – 7.62km (4.76 miles) – 265m ascent (869ft)
Princetown to Shipley Bridge – 19.64km (12.28 miles) – 305m ascent (1,000ft)
Shipley Bridge to South Brent – 3.83km (2.4 miles) 81m ascent (265ft).

Postbridge and Princetown at 17.6km and 33.6km (11 and 21 miles) respectively have visitor centres, inns, and shops to re-stock with supplies, and all the above have vehicular access should you decide you have had enough.

Trail shoes are a must on this and expect to get wet feet. Three miles or so in, there is a small river crossing and the first part of the route goes over wet moorland, even in the height of summer. Consider a spare pair of socks at Princetown.

Parking at Belstone, the start is best just north of the village, opposite the village hall, as there is a good deal of space and it is free.

Parking at South Brent is a bit more pot luck, although there is a free car park where the railway station used to be. It is often full however, so consider leaving a car in one of the nearby roads by the school.

Some may consider doing this at a more leisurely pace and split the route into two days. If that's your plan, then I would make the split at 21 miles and rest at Princetown which has numerous bunkhouses, inns and bed and breakfast establishments.

This route travels through the firing range near the beginning so make sure the range is clear and not firing on the day that you start this run.

Dartmoor guide – AF

It's a path ... honest! – AF

South of Redlake – AF

30 Dartmoor – Top to Bottom

Route

Section 1 – Belstone to Postbridge
South over the high moor via Belstone Tor, Oke Tor, Hangingstone Hill, Sittaford Tor before reaching the road at Postbridge. All off-road and over high ground.

Section 2 – Postbridge to Hexworthy
Through the forest, south to Bellever Tor, and then on to Hexworthy Bridge, over low-lying moorland.

Section 3 – Hexworthy to Princetown
Turn west after the bridge to follow the Dartmoor Way into Princetown.

Section 4 – Princetown to Shipley Bridge
South again along good tracks before crossing the River Plym at Plym Ford, and then following the Abbot's Way to Red Lake. Finish by following the River Avon via the Avon Dam and reservoir.

Section 5 – Shipley Bridge to South Brent
Pass over the River Avon and turn right to follow the valley south into South Brent via paths and lanes.

Detailed directions

Section 1 – Belstone to Postbridge

START Belstone village. Leaving the pub and village green behind, head out on a road, with the slopes of Belstone green to your left. The road is walled on the right, and soon bends right and then left past quaint houses. Take the right fork uphill to reach a large gate, and the entrance to the moor.

1 A wide stone track now appears upon passing through the gate and a split in the path is a few steps ahead, dominated by the view up to the heights of Belstone Common and Belstone Tor. Rather than take either track right or left, head straight on to climb on open moorland up to the ridge ahead. As this is a popular climb, an obvious trod is soon found, which winds its way up to the first crag. The going is steep, but easy and a good warm up for your legs.

2 Upon reaching the first summit, continue up to the next crag which is Belstone Tor. The view to the right over the high, moorland summits is worth a pause.

3 Follow the ridgeline towards the wall, and cross. Keep on the trod and ridgeline to make Higher Tor. The running is easy, although boulders litter the path so watch your step. The route now descends slightly and at another rocky outcrop, cross into the Okehampton Firing Range and follow the grassy trod slightly uphill now towards Oke Tor. If you stay on the broad ridge, you cannot really go wrong.

4 Pass Oke Tor on its left flank and then note the old and new range huts sheltering on the northernmost tip of the Tor. From here, the trod veers right slightly and gently downhill. There is another path that turns sharp right but ignore this. Instead head south still as the track becomes wider and more obvious.

5 This stone track, the remains of the old military roads, climbs gently and another track joins it from the right. Ignore this and continue onwards, past a telephone point on the left and eventually descend to cross a small river via a ford.

Dartmoor – Top to Bottom 30

Okement valley east – AF

❻ Keep going straight ahead, keeping left and climbing to one of the five highest peaks on Dartmoor, known as Hangingstone Hill. On top there is a small, metal range hut, turn half left here to pick up an obvious track which bends around the hillside and turns right to come out again on to open moor. This little, deep track is known as a peat pass, made to allow pedestrians to move across the moorland easily rather than bog-hopping. Those who now look right will see the previous range hut only a short distance away. The route around may seem longer but trust me, it is much quicker and less painful than wading through the bog which is situated between these two points.

❼ Turn left to follow the grassy trod down the centre of the ridge, aiming towards the next range huts known as Quintin's Man. On reaching this point, bear left to descend to a wall and use the line of this to follow a path down to a river crossing. Cross over and follow the wall line up to a wall junction, and cross the stile ahead on the left to access Sittaford Tor.

❽ Turn left towards the forest ahead and descend the quick path by the wall down to a pair of reconstructed stone circles known as The Grey Wethers. Turn right here and follow the path downhill, keeping the river on the right. I find it easier running to stay high up on the left, aiming for the top of Hartland Tor, so as not to lose height before having to climb again. The ground is generally drier the higher up you are.

❾ At the tor, head right and downhill to a fence line and find a gate in the corner next to the river. Go through and follow the path by the river initially, before turning left to follow the fence line around the edge of the field, turning right at the corner. Follow this path through a gate and on to the road. Turn right to cross the bridge into Postbridge and take a break, if you wish, at either the post office on the right, or the visitor centre further on, which has loos attached.

Section 2 – Postbridge to Hexworthy

❿ From the car park, cross the road and head across the cattle grid at the T-junction. Turn immediately right into a Forestry Commission car park. Go through and uphill, to the left, through a metal gate and head straight on up the hill, ignoring the path on the right. Follow this main path as it climbs before coming out on to open moorland before the climb to Bellever Tor.

11 From the top, go straight over the other side and head for the gate in the wall ahead. Once through, turn right to follow the track uphill to the corner of a wood. Cross through the wall and follow the path to the right of the woodland, to a gate that opens on to a road. Turn left on the road, being careful of traffic, and turn right at the next road on the right. Run down the hill, past a chapel on the left and all the way down to a bridge at Hexworthy and your next breather at the end of this section. The Forest Inn, just up the hill, may be open for refreshments.

Section 3 – Hexworthy to Princetown

12 Once ready to proceed, cross over the bridge and immediately turn right over a stile in the wall to ascend a steep, grassy hill. Follow the path across two fields before reaching a farm. Go through the farmyard and right, up a track to the right of the main house. Follow this to the top and at the road junction go straight ahead along a track. This bears right through fields following the line of a leat to the left, before descending to meet a footbridge.

13 Cross the river using the bridge and follow the path which is always wet. At the path junction turn left to follow through the remains of an old farmhouse and stables. The path is obvious, if narrow, and comes out on to open moorland via a gate. This is part of the Dartmoor Way and as such is well trodden. Ignoring all paths off to the left and right, stay straight on as it climbs. There are numerous water courses to cross at intervals and this, coupled with the uphill, makes for quite hard work. Eventually the path becomes a hard track and is easier to run along. The telegraph mast above Princetown is your guide ahead.

Note: The reason for the sudden appearance of the track is because this is the limit of how far the conscientious objectors got when building their road across the moor, during the First World War, while 'imprisoned' at Dartmoor Prison. If the weather is grim at this moment, I am sure a degree of sympathy might be forthcoming from we who exercise the right to run on such paths with freedom.

14 At the end, after a short downhill, turn right through the gate in front of Bullpark Farm and look for the plaque on the gatepost.

15 Follow the concrete road left, downhill, and then right at the bottom to head along a wide track with a stream on the left. Go through the gate and follow the track as it rises, and left to another gate. The track then flattens again and runs on to a fingerpost, with a track junction.

16 Turn left up the hill to a gate and cross the leat at the gate. Continue uphill to the top on the obvious track which swings right and then left to go around a plantation. The path then descends after another gate, past a house with a noisy collie. At the final gate by the house, go careful, as the path ends on a main road.

17 Turn left along the pavement and into Princetown. There is a public loo to the right of the Moorland Visitor Centre, cafés, and post office for refreshments. The pubs are also good here, but with fourteen miles still to go, a beer might not be the wisest of choices. For those stopping here, or doing this route over two days, fill your boots!

Dartmoor – Top to Bottom   30

Van support

Section 4 – Princetown to Shipley Bridge

18 At the mini roundabout outside the Princetown visitor centre, look for the track which goes to the left of the Plume of Feathers Inn. Pass through the gate and follow the stone track uphill. Passing through a second gate takes you on to open moorland, but still on a well-trodden / cycled stone track. The going is easy as you pass South Hessary Tor on the left, and numerous tracks begin to appear on both sides. Ignore these and carry straight on as it descends and a Dartmoor farmhouse, Nun's Cross Farm, appears on the left and the stone, Nun's Cross on the right.

19 Keep straight ahead on the main track as it climbs. As the path starts to descend, look out for some old ruins on the right and left, and take the track off to the left, which turns and descends almost back on yourself. Follow this downhill before swinging right to cross over the River Plym at a ford. The track now climbs uphill and is less obvious. This is known as the Abbot's Way, and eventually descends again into a valley with remnants of old mine workings. These are known as Erme Pits, and the path follows the line of a stream. The path bears left to leave the river and climbs up towards Red Lake where the ground can be marshy. With the disused tip, known locally as 'the volcano', on the left, follow the path to reach the main, disused railway at the Two Moors Way marker stone.

20 Turn right here to follow an obvious path up and around a small hill. Ignore the old tramway on the right, and instead bear left on the grassy path to descend steeply downhill towards the River Avon below. A faint trod leads down to a classic Dartmoor clapper bridge, which you must cross to continue the route.

21 Turn right after the bridge and pick up the uneven path following the line of the river downstream. The path here is often wet, and is very uneven, as the footfall, river and climate take its toll, so watch your step.

Eventually a small wall is crossed, and Huntingdon Cross is just on the other side. A small tributary comes in from the left, and time, weather and energy allowing, (it is nearly all downhill now to the finish) it's worth a quick visit to Keble's Chapel. Follow the right-hand side of the stream heading for the ruin. This is not the chapel. Once past the ruin, head to a small cluster of rocks, and just below this, between the rocks and the stream is the low depression of the chapel, marked with a small, crossed stone at one end. Retrace your steps back to the cross by the stream / river junction after your homage.

㉒ The path continues to follow the river downstream, and eventually a view of the Avon Dam Reservoir comes into view. The path skirts the left-hand side of the upper slopes of the body of water, and swings left to descend to a ford over a stream. After crossing, turn right and follow the banks of the reservoir, heading for the left-hand side of the dam. The brightly coloured life rings help in poor visibility here.

㉓ A stone track continues, down the left-hand side of the valley away from the dam, and again follows the line of the river. The track soon becomes a tarmac road, and makes for easy running down the valley, giving you a chance to recover and enjoy the view. This is a service road for the water authority, so rarely has traffic on it. The road crosses the river via a bridge and now follows the other bank. Notice the potential bathing spots and waterfalls on the left now.

㉔ Ignoring the road off to the right, keep following the river to a T-junction. A car park and loo are situated on the right, and an ice cream van can often be present, so make sure you carry some cash. This is Shipley Bridge and the end of the penultimate section.

Section 5 – Shipley Bridge to South Brent

㉕ Cross the bridge to the east via the road, and turn left here to cross the cattle grid and immediately take the waymarked footpath over a stile on the right, entering some woodland. The path is easy to follow now, and constant public footpath signs mark the way. Keep left and then eventually come out on a road. Go straight over, up a track past houses, and once through a gate, enter woodland again.

㉖ The path is now more a bridleway and descends to a ford before climbing, for the last time, up gentle slopes to a small hamlet. At the road junction turn right to follow the road downhill to another T-junction. Turn right here and head for the bridge over the River Avon. Turn left just before the bridge on to a footpath and head to the village of South Brent.

A less than obvious path

31 The Dartmoor 600s

Distance	24-32km (15-20 miles)
Ascent	Lots!
Grade	F3
Start / Finish	High Down car park SX 525 853 (50.6491 -4.0870)

Dartmoor is not known for its high mountains, yet it does have five tops over 600m (1,969ft) which are the highest in southern England. Not only that, they are also somewhat remote. Indeed, Cut Hill in the middle of the north moor, is some 3 miles from a road and can only be reached firstly by path, and then by covering a large amount of open moorland. It is argued by many that this is among one of the most remote spots in England and there is rarely anyone seen on its top. Unsurprising really when to get to it involves knee deep bog, large tussocks of tussock grass, or 'babies heads', and it is particularly uninspiring when there.

However, to the adventurous fell runner, getting to remote locations is part of the fun, but rather than just a venture out and back, I devised a circuit taking in the five highest peaks from a particular starting point. The five peaks in question are, going anti-clockwise: Cut Hill, Whitehorse Hill, Hangingstone Hill, High Willhays and Yes Tor.

This circuit has now developed into the Dartmoor 600s Challenge, and the aim of the game is to take in all the above tops in one continuous run, in any direction and order. The start point for this challenge is

31 The Dartmoor 600s

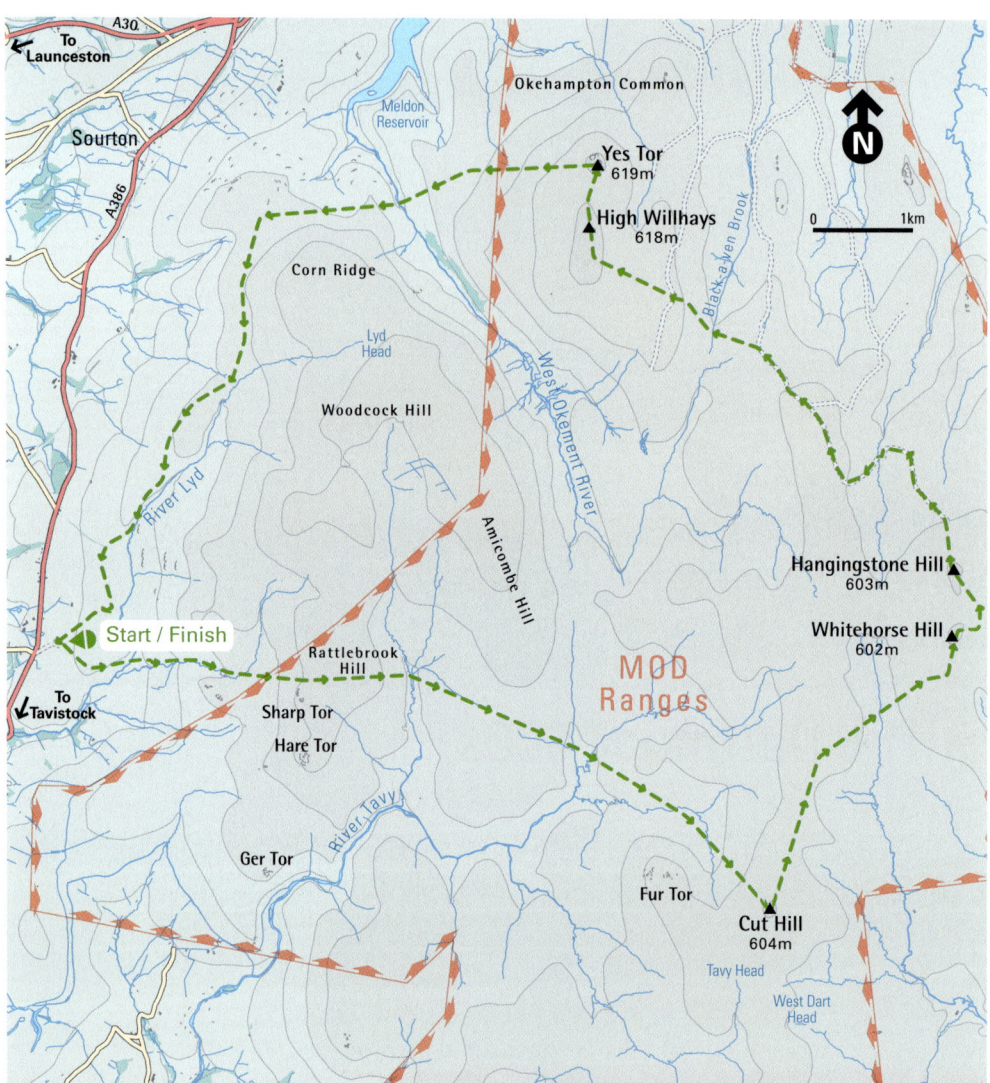

from a free car park on the west side of the moor, behind the Dartmoor Inn at Lydford. A track leads up to it through a gate on the left-hand side of the pub.

The route is entirely up to the individual and can be as direct or indirect as one likes. Navigation skills are essential, as is a day clear of live firing on the ranges as the route goes through two: Okehampton and Willsworthy Ranges.

On the route, there are rivers to cross and bogs to be avoided or negotiated.

The beauty of this challenge is that it is achievable for many, the distance being at its longest 20 miles, route dependant. However, the terrain is not to be underestimated, as the ground is often difficult to run over.

As this is a 2 hour plus circuit, give or take, I would suggest the minimum kit requirement as laid out in the introduction to the Longer Excursions section.

The Dartmoor 600s

Hangingstone Hill – RR

The Tops (in no particular order)

High Willhays
This is the highest and has a few pancake-style granite outcrops on its summit, one of which now has a small cairn.

Yes Tor
The tor is just a little north, along the flat ridge of High Willhays and has a trig point on the summit.

Hangingstone Hill
The hill has a large, flat summit with a metal range hut at its summit.

Whitehorse Hill
Whitehorse is few hundred yards from Hangingstone across broad, soggy peat hags. A handy peat pass is nearby and the sign at the southern end can be defined as the top of this broad, flat plain. There is little else to distinguish it.

Tavy Cleave

Follow the leader!

31 The Dartmoor 600s

At least it's dry. A good line from Cut Hill. – MBa

Cut Hill

This is a large mound, just east of Fur Tor. The top has a large depression and a small cairn to mark the top.

Notes

Before commencing this run:

- Check the ranges are clear.
- Make sure you can navigate in all weathers.
- Check the forecast. Heavy rain previous to the day of your run or during can cause the rivers to become unpassable.

Summit of High Willhays

Ridge between Yes Tor and High Wilhays

Index of Place Names

A
Abbot's Way 167, 172, 175
Aish Tor 136
Arms Tor 39, 40
Ashburton village 121
Ashburton village centre car park 121
Avon Dam Reservoir 143, 172, 176

B
Babeny clapper bridge 163
Babeny stepping stones 146
Badgers Holt café 135, 136, 164
Bag Tor 103
Ball Gate 141, 142
Becka Brook 116
Beckaford Bridge 116
Becky Falls 114
Bellever Forest 155
Bellever Forest car park 155, 163
Bellever Tor 7, 161, 162, 163, 172, 174
Bellever Woods 157, 158, 159, 163
Bell Tor 104
Belstone Common 56, 57, 172
Belstone Green 57, 172
Belstone Tor 57, 58, 172
Belstone village 55, 169, 171, 172
Bel Tor Corner 134
Bench Tor 133
Black-a-Tor Copse 32, 34, 36
Black Pool 128
Black Tor 29, 36, 70, 71, 72, 82, 83, 84, 166
Bonehill Rocks 89, 103, 104
Boulters Tor 50
Bovey Tracy 103
Bowerman's Nose 114, 115
Brat Tor 37, 40
Brent Tor 47
Broad Down 157, 158
Bullpark farm 149, 174
Burrator 85
Burrator Reservoir 69, 83, 87
Burrator Reservoir Dam 78, 85
Butterdon Hill 126, 128

C
Cadover Bridge 61
Cadover Cross 62, 63, 64
Cadworthy Tor 64
Café on the Green 109
Castle Drogo 91, 92, 94
Challacombe 111

Cherry Brook 159
Chinkwell Tor 104
Church House Inn 130
Cleave pub 116
Clifford Bridge 106
Combestone 135
Conchies Road 147, 148, 150
Coombe 94
Cosdon Beacon 58
Cosdon Hill 57, 58
Cowsic River 154
Cox Tor 43, 44, 47, 48
Cramber Tor 70, 72
Crazy Well pool 69, 70
Crockern Cottage 153
Cut Hill 177, 180

D
Dartmeet 135, 161, 162
Dartmoor Inn 76, 178
Dartmoor Inn Merrivale 41
Dartmoor National Park visitors centre 81
Dartmoor Prison 148
Dartmoor Way 167, 172, 174
Deadman's Corner 137
Devonport Cascade 83
Devonport Leat 71, 72, 81, 83, 150, 152, 153, 158
Dewerstone 61, 62, 63, 64
Dewerstone Iron Mine 62
Dewerstone store 81
Dinger Tor 33, 35
Ditsworthy Warren House 65, 66, 67
Dogmarsh Bridge 94
Dr Blackall's Drive 134, 136, 138
Drizzle Combe 65, 67

E
East Dart Hotel 155
East Dart River 157, 162, 163, 164
East Glaze Brook 142
East Okement River 169
Erme Pits 175
Eylesbarrow Tin Mine 68

F
Fingle Bridge 91, 92, 93, 108
Fingle Bridge Inn 91, 92
Fingle Woods 106, 107
firing ranges 11
Foggintor School 73

Index of Place Names

Forrest Inn 136
Four Winds car park 73
Fox and Hounds pub 37, 38
Fox Tor Café 81
Foxworthy hamlet 117
Fur Tor 180

G

Giant's Grave 105, 107
Godeswrthy 50
Granite Way 32
Great Combe Tor 47
Great Links Tor 37, 39
Great Mis Tor 43, 73, 74, 75
Great Nodden 39, 40
Great Staple Tor 43, 44, 47, 48
Greystone Rocks 103, 115
Grey Wethers 173
Grimspound 95, 96, 100, 111
Gutter Mire 66
Gutter Tor 66, 68, 77, 78, 79, 80, 87
Gutter Tor Refuge 65, 85, 87
Gutter Tor Refuge car park 65

H

Hamel Down 96, 109, 111, 112
Hameldown Beacon 110, 111
Hangershell Rock 128
Hangingstone Hill 172, 173, 177, 179
Harford Bridge 128
Harford hamlet 126, 128
Hartland Tor 157, 173
Hart Tor 60, 70, 72, 165
Haytor 97, 101, 103
Haytor Lower car park 101
Haytor Lowman 102
Haytor Rocks 102, 104
Headless Cross 106, 107
Heathercombe Farm 99
Heathercombe Woodlands 99
Hen Tor 67
Hexworthy 171, 172, 173, 174
Hexworthy Bridge 136, 172
Higher Down car park 177
Higher Hartor Tor 66, 67, 68
Higher Tor 172
Higher White Tor 157, 158
Higher Knowle Wood 116
High Moorland Visitor Centre 82
High Willhays 31, 33, 177, 179, 180
HMP Dartmoor 81
Holne Bridge 133
Holne Church 129, 131
Holne Moor 132

Holne Ridge 132
Holne village 130
Holwell Quarry 103
Holwell Tor 104
Homerton Hill 30
Hookney Tor 96, 97, 99, 111, 112
Hound Tor 58, 97, 100, 101, 103, 104, 114, 115
Hound Tor car park 95
Hunter's Path 93
Hunter's Tor 94
Hunters Tor 114, 115
Huntingdon Cross 143, 176

I

Ice Warrior gear shop 81
Ingra Tor 87
Irishman's Wall 56
Ivybridge 125, 126
Ivybridge Community College 127

J

Jay's Grave 95, 97, 100
Jobbers Lane 68

K

Keble's Chapel 141, 143, 176
Kestor Inn 113
King's Tor 85
King Tor 112

L

Langstone menhir 45, 46, 49
Laughter Tor 162, 163
Leather Tor 71, 84
Lime Street 108
Lints Tor 33, 35
Little Hound Tor 58
Little Mis Tor 75
Longaford Tor 153, 157, 158, 159
Lower Hartor Tor 67
Lower Hookner 99
Lower White Tor 157, 158
Lud Gate 132
Lustleigh Cleave 114
Lustleigh village 114, 116
Lydford 178
Lyd Valley 40

M

Manaton 115, 116, 118
Manaton Church car park 113
Manaton village 113
Mardon Down 106
Mariner's Way 99

Three Barrows 142
Top Tor 103, 104
Tors Inn 55
Two Bridges Hotel 151, 152
Two Moors Way 125, 126, 127, 128, 132, 137, 141, 142, 143, 167, 169, 175

V
Venford Dam car park 133
Venford Reservoir 137
Volcano 141

W
Warren House Inn 99
Water village 116
West Dart River 151, 152, 153, 158, 162
West Devon Way 29, 167
Western Beacon 126, 127
West Okement River 29, 35
White Hart Inn 107
White Hill 43
Whitehorse 177, 179
White Moor Stone Circle 56, 57, 58
White Thorn pub 63
White Tor 43, 44, 47, 49, 50
Widecombe 112
Widecombe in the Moor (village) 103, 109
Widecombe village green 109
Widgery Cross 37
Willingstone Rock 108
Willsworthy Firing Range 178
Wistman's Wood 151, 153, 154, 158
Wooston Castle 106, 108

Y
Yar Tor 135, 136, 164
Yartor Down 136
Yes Tor 33, 34, 52, 53, 177, 179

Index of Place Names

Meavy village 78, 85
Meavy village green 77
Meldon dam 29, 33
Meldon Reservoir 27, 29, 31, 36
Meldon Reservoir car park 27, 31
Merrivale 41, 75
Merrivale Firing Range 45, 47
Merrivale Quarry 41, 73, 76
Merrivale Stones 75, 76
Michelcombe 131
Middle Staple 41
Moorland Visitor Centre 174
Moretonhampstead 105, 107

N
New Bridge 133, 135
Nodden Gate 40
Norsworthy Bridge car park 69, 70
North Hessary 83
North Hessary Tor 76, 82
North Wood 64
Nun's Cross 83, 87, 175
Nun's Cross Farm 82, 83, 85, 87, 175

O
Okehampton 51, 52
Okehampton Firing Range 31, 55, 58, 172, 178
Okement valley 32, 35
Okement valley east 173
Oke Tor 58, 172
Old Inn 109
Old Lych Way 46
Old railway station, South Brent village 139
Old School Tea Room 55
Oxen Tor 63, 64

P
Peat Cot Farm 149, 150
Peter Tavy 45
Peter Tavy Church 45
Peter Tavy Inn 47
Plume of Feathers Inn 83, 86, 147, 149, 175
Plym Ford 172
Postbridge 155, 161, 162, 164, 171, 172, 173
Postbridge visitors car park 155
Powdermills 158
Primrose tearoom 116
Prince of Wales Inn 81
Princetown 81, 85, 88, 147, 171, 172, 174, 175
Princetown visitor centre 147
Puffing Billy Track 141
Pupers Hill 129, 131

Q
Quickbeam Hill 143

R
Raven's Tor 114
Red Lake 142, 143, 172, 175
Ringmoor Cottage 80
Rippon Tor 103, 104
River Avon 140, 141, 142, 143, 144, 172, 175, 176
River Bovey 114, 116
River Dart 133, 134, 135, 136
River Erme 125, 128
River Lyd 39
River Meavy 71, 83
River Plym 63, 64, 67, 172, 175
River Teign 91, 93, 106, 108
River Walkham 42, 43, 75
Roos Tor 43, 47, 49, 74, 75
Rowtor 53
Royal Oak Inn 77, 78
Rugglestone Inn 103, 109
Run Venture Ltd 4
Ryder's Hill 129, 130, 131, 132

S
Scary Tor 52, 53
Scorriton hamlet 131, 132
Sharpitor 114, 115, 117
Sharp Tor 93, 135, 136, 160
Sharrah Pool 137
Shaugh Prior 63
Shaugh Prior village 64
Sheeps Tor 78, 80, 83
Shipley Bridge 9, 141, 142, 171, 172, 175, 176
Simmonds Park 51, 52, 53
Sittaford Tor 172, 173
Smeardon Down 47, 50
Snowdon 129, 131, 132
Soussons Wood 162
South Brent Manor 141
South Brent village 139, 141, 144, 169, 171, 172, 176
South Hessary Tor 82, 83, 87, 149, 175
South Zeal village 58
Spitchwick Manor 134
Steeperton Gorge 56, 57
Steeperton Tor 57, 58
Stephen's Grave 47, 50
Stowford Paper Mill 125, 128

T
Tavy Cleave 47, 179
Tavy Valley 49
Teign Valley 106
The Forest Inn 174